DRAWING
AND PAINTING
RACING
CARS

DRAWING
AND PAINTING
RACING
CARS

Michael Turner shows you how

Title page: Baron Emmanuel de Graffenried in his Maserati 4CLT at the British Grand Prix, 1949, which he went on to win.

© 1999 Michael Turner

First published in 1999

A catalogue record for this book is available from the British Library

ISBN 1 85960 627 X

Library of Congress catalog card no. 99-73266

Published by Haynes Publishing, Sparkford, Nr Yeovil, Somerset BA22 7JJ, UK.

Tel. 01963 440635 Fax 01963 440001
Int. tel. +44 1963 440635 Fax +44 1963 440001
E-mail: sales@haynes-manuals. co. uk
Web site: www.haynes.co.uk

Haynes North America, Inc.,
861 Lawrence Drive, Newbury Park,
California 91320, USA

Typeset by G&M,
Raunds, Northamptonshire
Printed and bound in England by
J. H. Haynes & Co. Ltd, Sparkford

Contents

Introduction

It was in the late 1960s that Patrick Stephens asked me if I would write a book on 'how to draw cars'. I had known Pat when he was Advertisement Manager for *Motor Racing* and we had travelled together to places such as Le Mans when I was providing sketches of events for the magazine. He had recently left to form his own publishing company (PSL), and I was flattered to be considered as a potential author on my particular subject. True, there weren't many alternatives available, but I was still a relative newcomer to the professional scene. This fact did cause me to have some misgivings, however, and I felt that my relative lack of know-how would deprive such a work of the authority it should command. I was also very busy, and my first commitment was to the deadlines which were of prime importance when building up a career.

The project was therefore put on hold, although I did in fact produce a synopsis, a rough design for the cover, and a sample chapter. I don't quite know where the time went, but in spite of periodic reminders from Pat over the intervening 30 plus years, during which time his company flourished, was three times merged with larger publishing groups, and moved from London to Cambridge to Northants and then to Somerset, the book remained something of a 'sleeper'.

Apart from Patrick, I have known his former partner Darryl Reach, now Editorial Director of the Haynes, Special Interest Publishing Division, since he joined the original company. The book, which had become something of an in joke between the three of us, was again put forward for consideration recently. I realised that, at the age of 65, and after more than 40 years of making a living from drawing and painting motorsport, I was as ready as I ever would be to pontificate on some of the experience I should by now be qualified to pass on.

When I was still at school, my parents gave me a little book called *How to Draw Cars* by the late Frank Wootton. That book, together with a companion title, *How to Draw 'Planes* by the same artist, provided me with the initial inspiration and pointers which encouraged me into what became a consuming and satisfying career. Since then, there has been very little similar available to provide guidance to aspiring artists with an interest in cars, or the countless people who want to try to extend their artistic interest by having a go, or even just understand a little of what is behind pictures which they enjoy looking at.

Because of the tremendous increase in interest in motor racing, and the fact that most of my work connected with cars has been directed at the motorsport scene, we decided that the concept of the book should now concentrate on this aspect alone, and not generalise on cars of all sorts. The principles are of course the same as far as the portrayal of machines with wheels are concerned, but there are so many facets to interpreting and conveying the excitement of the speed and action inherent in motor racing that it was felt there was more than enough material in this specialised aspect of the subject on which to concentrate.

My enthusiasm for motorsport has taken me all over the world, gathering information and experiences in my quest to do justice, both artistically and historically, to this dramatic activity. Like most artists, I am my own sternest critic, and inevitably therefore the results of my labours always fall short of my hopes, and some fall shorter than others, but it is this shortfall that is necessary to promote the determination to do better. I hope of course that my artistic abilities have nevertheless improved with the passage of time, but because I have always seen things as they are, my work is a mixture of the representational and the impressionistic.

While the action and atmosphere of motorsport are a prime motivating factor for me, machines have a functional presence, and to my eye the components have to conform to their designed shape and form even when interpreted in the exciting environment they inhabit. This may not be a view acceptable to everyone of course, but it is mine and therefore the underlying approach put forward in this book. Whatever is done in the name of art,

if the bases of good draughtsmanship and observation are flouted or ignored to an unacceptable degree, then I question the validity of the result. This is not to say that abstract images are beyond my appreciation – far from it – but the ones I admire are artistically sound and have an underlying sense of colour, design or technique which are instantly recognisable and usually founded on solid academic principles.

Whatever your particular criteria, and whether your interest is that of a doer or a viewer, I hope that there will be something useful to be gleaned from the following pages. At least the long period of gestation has considerably increased the choice of examples available since conception!

Michael Turner,
Chesham, Bucks, 1999

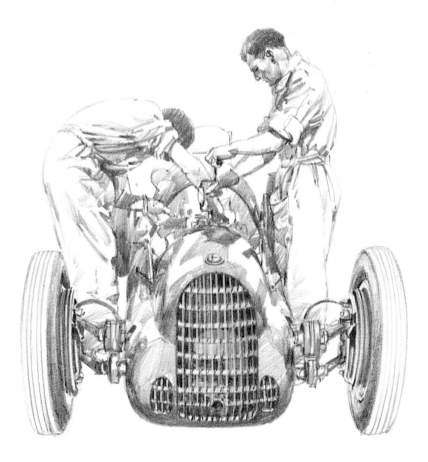

Alfa Romeo 158 (1938).

Chapter One

Drawing materials and equipment

The good news is that to embark on a trial session of drawing, you do not need to commit yourself to much of an outlay in monetary terms. The most basic tools needed to make a start with some exploratory drawing are, not surprisingly, a pencil and some paper. However, it will come as no surprise to learn that there is a considerable choice of grades and types of both of these items, so let's get some idea of the options available.

Lead pencils come in a variety of grades which denote the softness or hardness of the lead. These classifications use 'H' to denote hard grades, and 'B' to denote soft grades. In between these we have 'HB', a neutral position, with the hard grades getting harder as they progress through H, 2H, 3H, 4H etc, and the soft grades getting softer through B, 2B, 3B, 4B, 5B, and 6B, generally the softest and blackest of the range. Unless you are intending to do fine detailed line work, I suggest you ignore anything with an H suffix, as for sketching you need only consider using B grades. The softer the lead, the quicker it will wear down, so a good starting grade would be 2B, with a 4B and 6B for more general shading and where you need some nice juicy black tones.

The inconvenience of frequent sharpening and shorter life is compensated for by richness of tone and the ability to cover larger areas more easily. Personally, I rarely use a pencil harder than a 2B, but if you feel happier with a more precise result, the expense of experiment until you establish your preferences is not a bank breaker.

In addition to conventional lead pencils, there are softer graphite pencils which provide an even darker tone, but they have a slightly 'waxy' nature which gives a different feel, but which can be very satisfying for loose sketching.

Softer still is charcoal, and while sticks of this material are cheap and broad, satisfying tonal effects can be achieved, it is a messy medium and requires a more intuitive application and approach.

However, to cater for those who don't like the idea of getting their fingers dirty and transmitting fingermarks to everything they touch, charcoal is also available in pencil form, although the wooden cladding does incur a greater cost than when it is in its natural state.

Pastel and conte-crayon are sticks of compressed powder and, like charcoal, are messy to handle even by the more meticulous amongst us, but can equally be very rewarding to use, especially on tinted paper. Coloured pastels will be spoken of in a later section, but monotone greys, browns, sepia and terracotta are available in various grades of softness and, being unclad, can be used along their length to cover a broad area with few strokes – a great help when shading background tones. By breaking the sticks to form a sharp edge, fine lines can also be achieved for indicating detail. It is possible to use the

sticks in holders, which keeps the fingers cleaner, but this, as with charcoal pencils, rather destroys the opportunity to take advantage of their different characteristics compared with those of the lead pencil. As with charcoal, you will need to protect your work from smudging by your own hands while working, and a piece of flimsy paper can be placed over the vulnerable parts of the drawing for this purpose.

Personally, I have never really got along with line drawing using a pen and Indian ink, as I find it difficult to achieve the variety of tone and feel to suit my approach and objectives. This doesn't mean that you should not try it at some stage, and it can be combined with tone washed on with a brush and watercolour to achieve some very pleasing and satisfactory results. The felt pen and marker come somewhere between the pen and pencil, and favour a looser technique, at the same time allowing

a reasonable variation in line quality. However, bear in mind that these media are instantly permanent and therefore less forgiving, requiring a confident approach and advance appreciation of the result you hope to produce.

First though, concentrate on the pencil, before venturing into other options. Pencils need to be sharpened from time to time, and I find a Stanley knife with replaceable blades ideal for this task. Pencil sharpeners can be all right for the harder grades of lead, but I prefer the knife blade as it gives greater flexibility for deciding on the length of lead available for shading. Bear in mind that softer grades of lead break more easily, and you will see your investment rapidly disappearing into the waste bin unless your blades are very sharp. The knife also allows

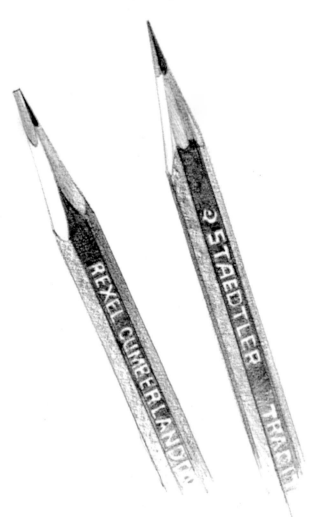

you to sharpen the lead to a chisel point, which will provide a useful combination of flat side for shading and fine edge for detail. To obtain this, you need to place the point of the lead on a flat surface, preferably not your best dining table, and shave the rounded lead flat on two sides.

As with charcoal and pastel, albeit to a lesser extent, it is easy to smudge your drawing while working, so you may want to protect your work from the attentions of your moving hand by introducing a piece of scrap paper. This is only really practical when using a drawing board, where the scrap is not prone to falling away, and if necessary it can be lightly secured with masking tape. When you have finished, it is a good idea to 'fix' your drawing for posterity and to protect it from accidental smudging. Fixative is available in easy-to-use aerosol spray cans, but remember that once fixed it will be too late to make corrections by rubbing out.

You will make mistakes, certainly until you gain confidence, and one way out is to erase the errors rather than start over again. Unless you are working on a hard surface, avoid those rubbers we used to use at school, often provided as an extension on the ends of pencils, or in rectangular slabs, as they will only result in ugly smears and damage the surface of the paper. It would be better to deny yourself the comfort of an eraser totally, leaving the misplaced line or overworked area to act as an incentive to do better, but if you do need a means of eliminating minor aberrations, then use a kneadable rubber, or 'putty rubber' as they are known in the trade.

These are pliable substances, and when warmed in the palm of the hand can be moulded into various shapes and are often useful for getting at small sections without obliterating adjacent and satisfactory lines. The unwanted lead or charcoal will stick to it and lift off the surface according to the amount of pressure applied, and whereas it will not always remove every trace of the offending stroke, it will do well enough to apply correction. Do not try to use the same piece for too long as it will become saturated with accumulated lead and cry 'enough', transferring the unwanted smudges back on to your work with

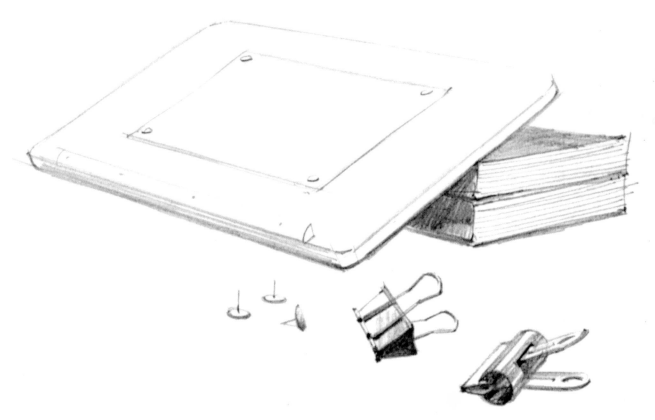

unhappy results. No doubt you will discover this for yourself, as have we all! You can also use the putty rubber for picking out highlights on pencil or charcoal drawings or for cleaning out areas and creating sharp edges between tones, useful assets for putting the finishing touches to a sketch.

The choice of drawing paper will also affect the results you achieve, smoother surfaces favouring softer leads, and rougher textures a harder lead. Use a fairly smooth paper for your initial trials, but don't invest in a large sketch pad, which can be wasteful of resources if you don't find it satisfactory, as a small A5-size pad or some single sheets of differing surfaces from your local art store will be adequate. Try some shading to find out how smooth or coarse the results are, then go for the one you feel happiest with.

One of my favourite surfaces for sketching is layout paper over which the pencil glides smoothly and evenly, but being only flimsy and semi-transparent it lacks substance if you are intending to produce a drawing of saleable quality. Pads of layout paper are less expensive than cartridge, and will provide an economical supply of paper, particularly as you can tear out and throw away the attempts which go horribly wrong without the anguish of assessing the cost of each sheet as it goes into the bin. Another benefit of layout paper is that you can progress a drawing which has gone slightly wrong by placing it under a fresh sheet and, being able to see the image through the paper, work over the existing lines, correcting errors and proportions as you go. This is particularly useful when working out various compositional ideas for a prospective painting.

If you use single sheets of paper, rest them on an even surfaced board or thick card, but be warned that any irregularity in the surface of this will leave an irremovable impression on any shaded area. You may find it advantageous to secure your paper to the drawing board or working surface by using drawing pins or spring clips (bulldog, etc).

Chapter Two

Perspective

One of the most baffling artistic puzzles for many people is how to convey a three-dimensional object or scene on a one-dimensional piece of paper or flat surface. The secret lies in an understanding and employment of the rules of perspective. When we see a three-dimensional object in space, its appearance and the angle at which it is presented to the viewer is governed by our position relative to it and the horizon. Theoretically, if there were an uninterrupted view across a desert, the line where the sand and sky meet would be our horizon. If we raise ourselves to a higher level, the horizon will also be higher, and we will see more sand and less sky.

Conversely, if we sit down, the horizon will be lower and we will see less sand and more sky.

In reality, a view of the horizon will usually be obscured at least in part by objects and obstructions between it and the viewer, but it will still be there, way off in the distance, and has to be borne in mind when setting the viewpoint. The most common demonstration of simple perspective, which I feel sure you will recall from school art classes, is that of a railway track leading into the distance, the parallel rails appearing to converge as they get further away until they meet at the horizon. Unfortunately, few objects are composed of

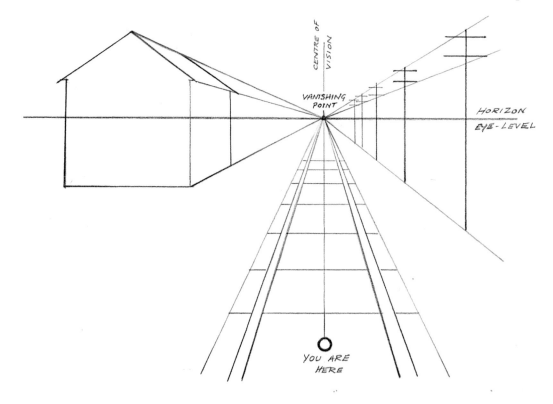

straight lines placed at right angles to the horizon, so we have to establish vanishing points where projections of major objects, sometimes on different planes, appear to meet. Remember that there will still be only one horizon, which will be at your eye-level, and if you look down on something from above, it will be below the horizon, and if you are looking up at an object, it will be above the horizon.

Perspective is all around us – sit near a rectangular table and see how the edges relate to your position. Look beyond and to each side, and notice how horizontal lines converge from above and below, and from side to centre. Doorways and shelves, books and chairs alter their relative perspective as you move your eye-level around. There will be some slight change to verticals, but for most purposes you can consider that these remain constant unless you are looking up or down at a steep angle. In this case your horizon will no longer relate to a normal eye-level, but become an arbitrary one related to your line of vision.

Draw any basic object and you will see how it relates to your viewpoint and eye-level. If you take a panoramic view, you will notice that, as you look from left to right, the horizontals will taper away to their own distant vanishing points each side of straight ahead. This is a situation where so-called artistic licence can come into play, but something you need not consider at this stage.

You will notice in the example of simple perspective that the vertical telegraph poles, which are in reality the same distance apart, get visually closer together as their distance from you increases, diminishing progressively in the same way that the horizontal distance between the railway lines decrease towards the horizon. This phenomenon is one of the fundamental rules of perspective, and you will appreciate that this is demonstrated when you look at any similarly-sized objects placed at varying distances from you – the further away they are, the smaller they appear to be. Remember that the closer you are to the subject, the more noticeable will be the effects of perspective.

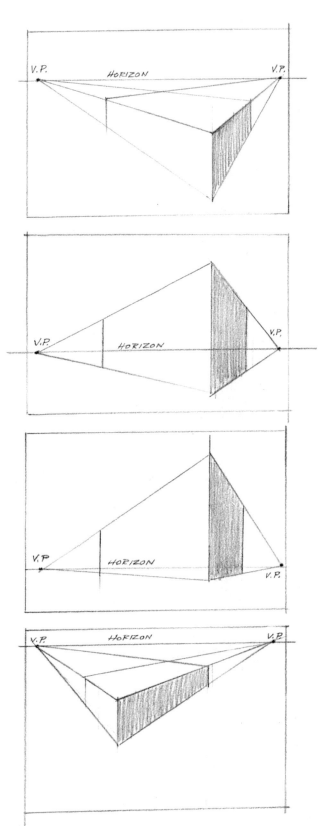

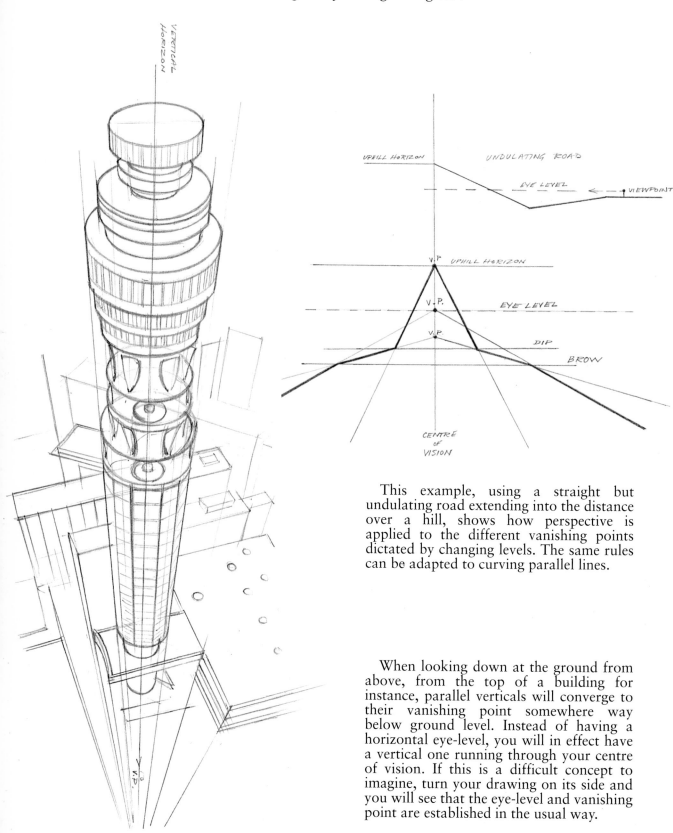

This example, using a straight but undulating road extending into the distance over a hill, shows how perspective is applied to the different vanishing points dictated by changing levels. The same rules can be adapted to curving parallel lines.

When looking down at the ground from above, from the top of a building for instance, parallel verticals will converge to their vanishing point somewhere way below ground level. Instead of having a horizontal eye-level, you will in effect have a vertical one running through your centre of vision. If this is a difficult concept to imagine, turn your drawing on its side and you will see that the eye-level and vanishing point are established in the usual way.

Perspective

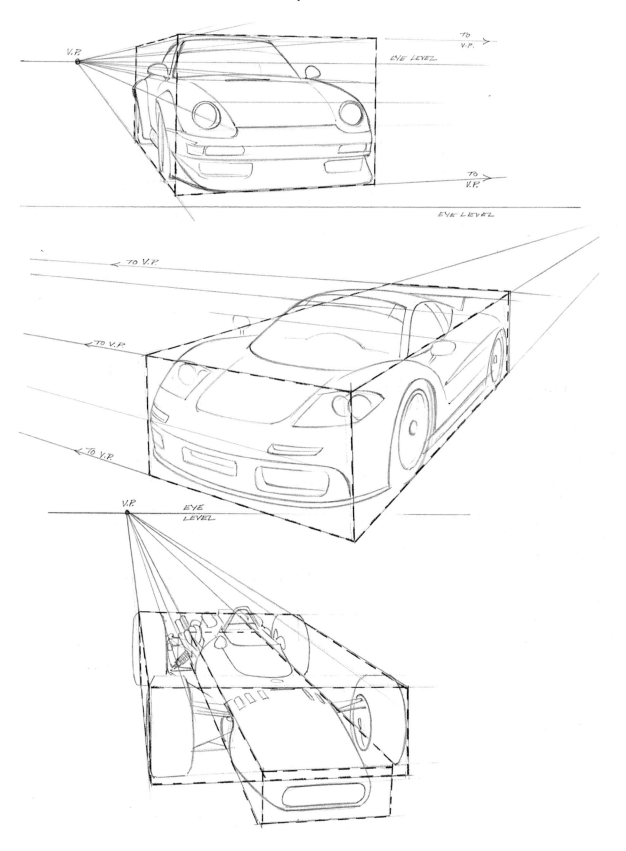

15

1983 Le Mans 24 Hours, with the works Porsche of Vern Schuppan blasting down the Mulsanne Straight past Les Hunaudières restaurant.

The concept of parallel lines of perspective converging towards the distant horizon is easy to follow in this painting, where even the building featured on the left is conveniently rectangular and simple in construction, as well as being placed parallel to the road. As if that wasn't help enough, the Armco barrier on the right also conforms to the simplest application of the basic rules.

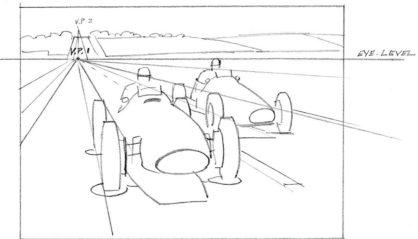

1953 French Grand Prix – Mike Hawthorn in the Ferrari challenges Fangio's Maserati as the pair approach Thillois Hairpin on the last lap of their thrilling duel for the lead. Hawthorn passed Fangio to win as they crossed the finish line.

The long straight at Reims also provides a good example of the application of basic perspective. The only slight complication is that the road goes uphill in the distance, so there are in effect two vanishing points which apply to the otherwise straight road as it disappears over the horizon.

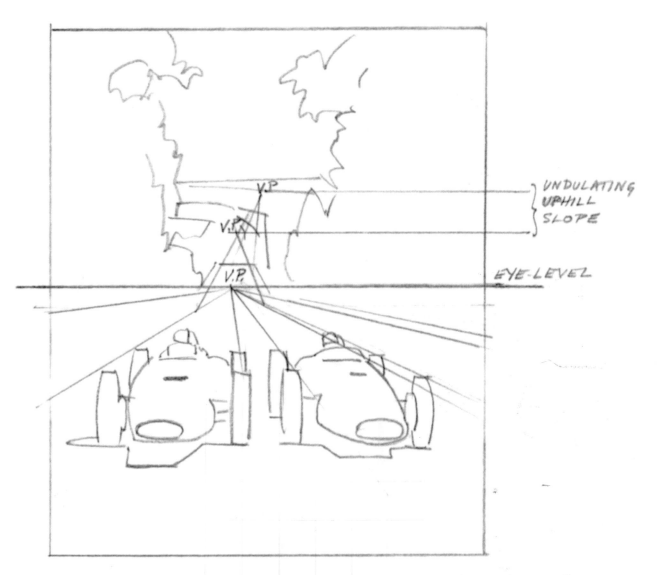

The 1957 German Grand Prix on the famous Nürburgring. Mike Hawthorn and Peter Collins, leading the race in their Ferraris, exchange worried signals as Fangio's Maserati reels them in down the straight leading to the start-finish area. He took the lead on the following lap to win after an epic drive.

Although the track is slightly curving in this picture as it heads off into the distance, the effect of perspective is still obvious – all you need to do is pull the vanishing point of the track in a slightly different direction while continuing to taper the sides together. The undulations where the track gradient changes require slightly different vanishing points, as in the picture on the previous page, and these establish the up and downhill nature of the track. The hedge which runs alongside the track is consistent in height, and therefore also conforms to the same perspective vanishing points. You will notice that the trees, although not all of the same height, diminish in size proportionally in relation to their distance from the viewer.

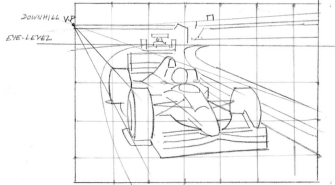

1993 British Grand Prix. Johnny Herbert cranks his Lotus through the exit from Stowe Corner at Silverstone ahead of Patrese's Benetton during their battle for third place towards the end of the race.

Slightly more complicated than the previous examples, the track here curves away quite sharply, with a gradient put in for good measure, but having established the horizon line the other objects all relate to this datum. The grandstands in the background are placed at varying angles to the viewpoint, so you will note the variations in the vanishing points which apply. The grandstand to the left is pretty well at right-angles to the viewer, so there is virtually no perspective taper on the roof line, but the right-hand grandstand, being at an angle to the viewer, does show the effects of perspective relative to its vanishing point. The foreground car is being looked down on because it is on a gradient, so its vanishing point extends to a point above the basic horizon of the general view.

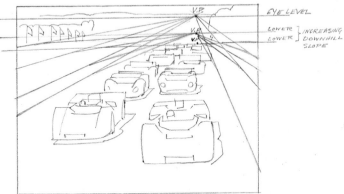

The Can-Am field thunders away at Elkhart Lake in 1970, with Denny Hulme and Bruce McLaren showing the way as expected.

Back to a relatively straightforward perspective example again, except that this time the track dips downhill out of sight into the valley in the middle distance. Consequently, you are looking at the cars at a progressively lower eye-level as they get further away, because the track they are on is at a changing angle. Nevertheless, the principle eye-level for the picture remains coincident with the distant horizon. It will be noticed that the distance between the uprights of the pits on the left get closer together as they get further away, as described in the basic rules of perspective.

Chapter Three

Ellipses

No matter what method of propulsion is employed, from elastic bands to jet turbine, without wheels our car would not get very far. Ideally, these wheels should be round, and when viewed face-on the wheel is of course a circle. An artist looking for an easy way out can stick a compass point on the paper and produce a perfectly circular wheel, but as we all know, life is not that straightforward. The scope for a budding automotive artist would be limited indeed if he or she were unable to draw a wheel at any of its infinitely variable attitudes.

The mastery of the ellipse, for this is what a circle becomes when viewed from an angle, seems to pose more of a problem than most other aspects of car illustration, but there is a relatively easy means at hand to help us understand the fundamental principles involved. Imagine a circular disc cut out of a piece of stiff material such as card or metal. Through the centre of this disc and at right angles to it runs an axle – a convenient term in view of this particular application – and at right angles to this axle is the axis, whose length determines the maximum dimension of the wheel. As we turn the disc towards or away from us, the circle ceases to appear round, and the width of the resulting ellipse varies according to the angle of view. If you mark off the width you require to suit your chosen viewpoint, using equal lengths each side of the centre point along the axle as a datum, you can join the four points with identical curves. Try to avoid any lumps, or pointy bits at the top and bottom of the

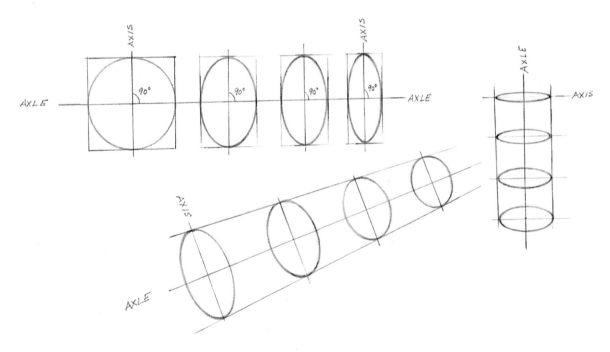

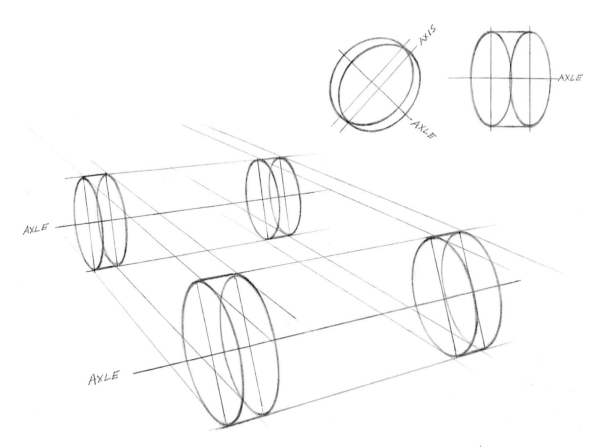

resultant ellipse if you want a smooth ride. By dividing an ellipse up in this way, it should make the task of producing a symmetrical shape easier.

If this still sounds difficult after studying the examples shown, then draw a circle on a square piece of card, divide it up into quarters, pierce it in the centre with a pin and observe it from various viewpoints. You may notice that if the ellipse is viewed from more extreme angles when perspective will affect the shape of the encompassing square, the axis will move slightly from the perceived centre, but don't let this fine-tuning confuse you. The effects are minimal and not enough of a factor to bother about in most normal circumstances.

All being well, we now know how to draw a round disc at different angles. To construct a simple wheel merely requires a second disc to be positioned on the same axle, but using a separate axis placed at a suitable distance to represent the width of the wheel in relation to its size.

However, just as you thought all this was looking easy, the effect of perspective comes into play. Looking at two wheels at either end of a common axle, you will see the closer one has a narrower ellipse than the one further away because of the convergence of the perspective lines by which they are governed. This is where the judgement of your eye will be critical, for the endless use of mathematical formulae can be time-consuming and self-defeating.

I often employ a little constructive imagination when visualising an object in three dimensions, and it may also help if you mentally position your basic wheel discs on hubs in your constructional drawing in the same way that you would mount or remove a real wheel from a vehicle.

Using the same principle, you can progress to giving your wheel a profiled tyre, which is simply a build-up of ellipses on the common axle related to the contours of the moulding. Not an easy concept to explain in words, but reference to the accompanying sketches should provide enlightenment.

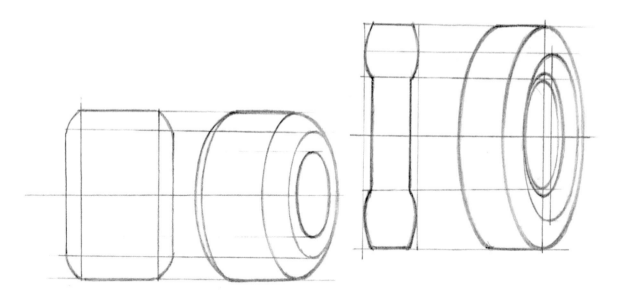

Obviously, to enable a vehicle to deviate from a straight course, cars have to have steerable wheels, usually at the front end. To draw wheels which are turned at an angle to the chassis, pivot the axles at the king-pins, in the same way that they would function in reality, and construct your ellipses in the desired position.

One more item to further complicate the whole business is the question of camber angles. The front wheels of cars are usually set at a slight angle from the vertical to assist the steering geometry. On early cars, this was quite noticeable – particularly where beam axles were employed. The latest breed of Formula One cars have gone to the other extreme and the front wheels are cambered in towards the top. Some racing cars have rear wheels which are set off the vertical, and these can change their angle under the effects of acceleration. To cope with these characteristics you need to set your axle and related axis accordingly.

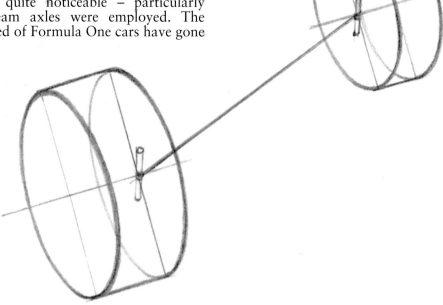

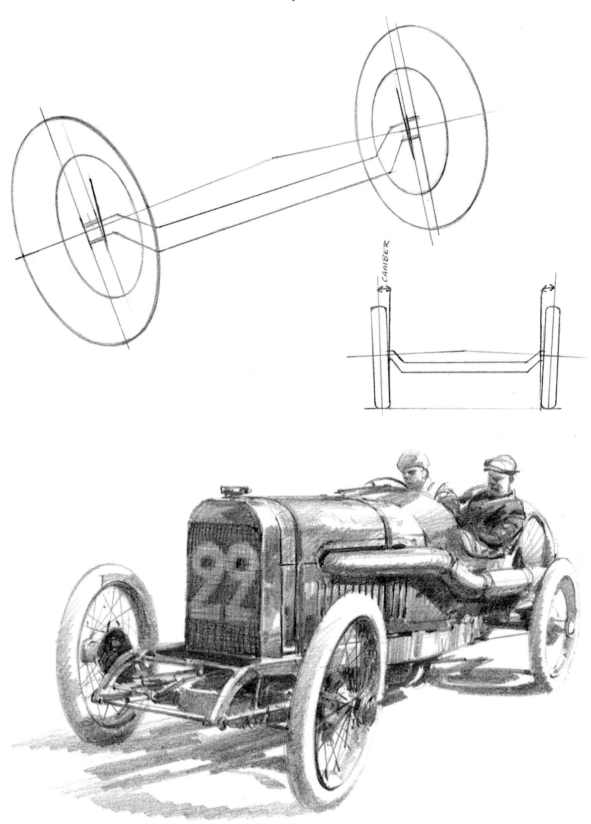

CAMBER

BUGATTI

P3 FILLER

OIL COOLER
ALFA

Ellipses

Still working with the ellipse in relation to wheels and tyres, we can continue along the same lines to build up brake drums, discs, etc. In addition, there are many other applications of ellipses connected to car drawing, and you will be able to employ them when drawing ancillaries such as steering wheels, filler caps, wheel spinners, exhausts and the infinite mass of paraphernalia which abounds in pit-stop and garage scenes.

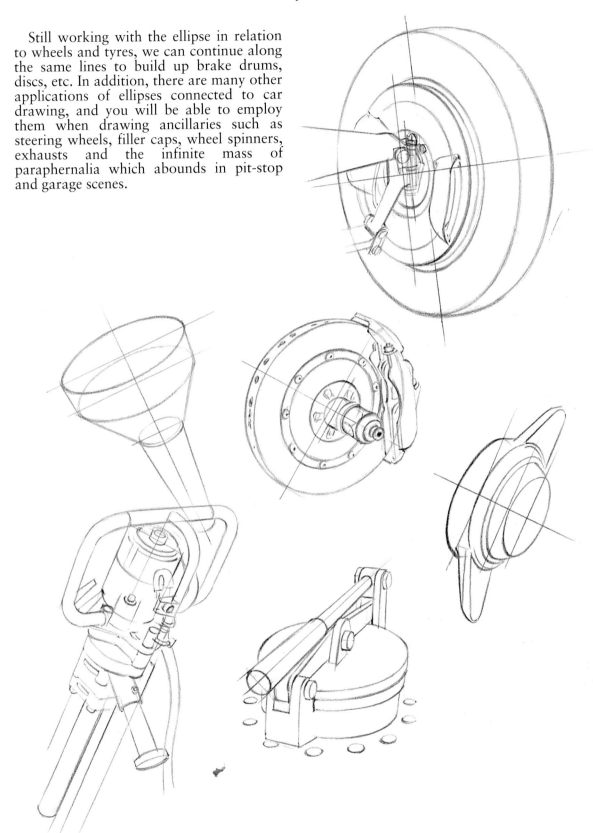

Chapter Four

Construction and proportion

If cars were built as simple box shapes with straight sides, tops and ends, with a wheel at each corner as they tended to be in the early days, (before the advent of advanced materials, modern engineering and construction methods, aerodynamics and styling, and all the sophistication we have become accustomed to), you should now be able to make a reasonable attempt at drawing a car. Unfortunately, because of all these developments they are not like this, so when confronted by a sleek, curvy and functional object such as a racing car, shaped to perform with maximum efficiency for the intended task of going as quickly as possible, we are once more at a bit of a loss as to where to start. Well, in

spite of all those curves and tapers, you will be relieved to learn that underneath them all there still lurks the basic box shape.

Being a keen modeller from an early age, I often found it useful to imagine starting with a block of wood of suitable dimensions from which to carve a three-dimensional model of my chosen vehicle. If you were to draw a side elevation of the required shape on the side of the block, and a plan view on the top, you could carve away the unwanted bits of wood to produce your basic shape, further improving and refining it by whittling away the other more subtle parts until you have before you the shape representing the overall appearance of the car. This works in

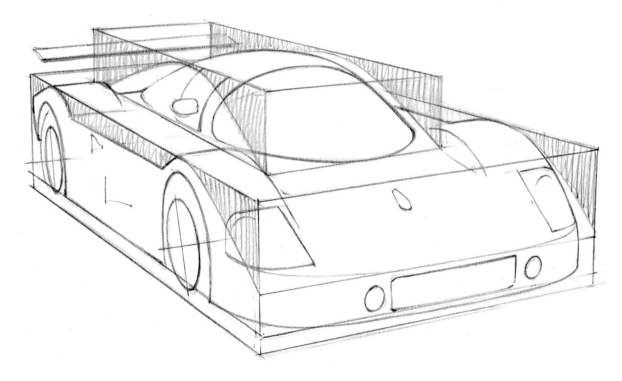

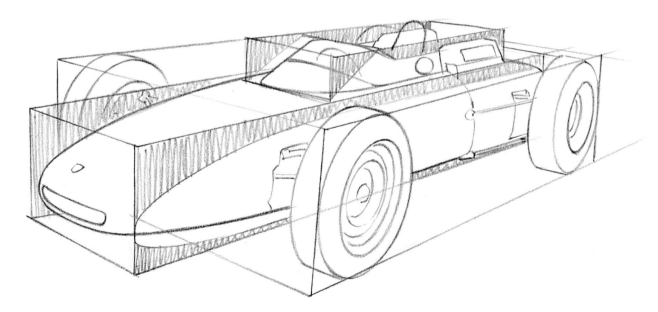

its simplest form on a conventional road-going car, or an enclosed sports car, but with a bit of imagination it can be equally adapted to encompass an open-wheeler.

If you have difficulty in getting started, you can try this approach, which I am confident will help in understanding the three-dimensional form involved and thereby overcome this initial obstacle to progress. The advantage of this method is that you can establish your viewpoint and aspect of the car using a basic block before wasting a lot of time drawing it out and then wanting to change the angle. When applying the principle to open wheeled racing cars, you can place a wheel at each corner and use these points to locate the shape within, linking suspension arms to pick-up points on the body, etc. This will also help you to establish height and position of projecting bodywork and other extremities and their relation to the overall subject. You will have to develop your own judgement of proportion, as it would be tedious and unhelpful to get bogged down in actual measurements. These will in any case vary on anything viewed from an angle as the distance from viewpoint increases, but it is not too difficult to relate wheel height to track width, for instance, until it looks right. Incidentally, bear in mind that on competition cars, particularly

single-seaters, the widths of the front and rear tracks are often different, as are the overall circumferences and widths of front and rear tyres.

This method enables you to find the simplest breakdown of what can sometimes be complex forms and double curvatures, all of which affect the appearance of a car when viewed from different angles. If you can relate the shapes to component blocks, you should find it easier to make headway. The examples of both racing and sports cars shown here will help to establish the principle in your mind. Try applying it to any vehicle which is accessible to you, or, if you prefer to work this one out in the comfort of your home, model cars can be a very useful and appropriate substitute.

It is of course important that you get the proportions of your subject correct in the essential areas, as the relationship of the various curved and flat surfaces when viewed from different angles will affect the overall impression and make the result convincing or otherwise. As a quick check, use your finger and thumb on the stem of your pencil to roughly measure the height of a wheel on the car, model or photograph you are using as a reference, and see how many times this divides into the track or some other measurable feature. You can then apply the same calculations to

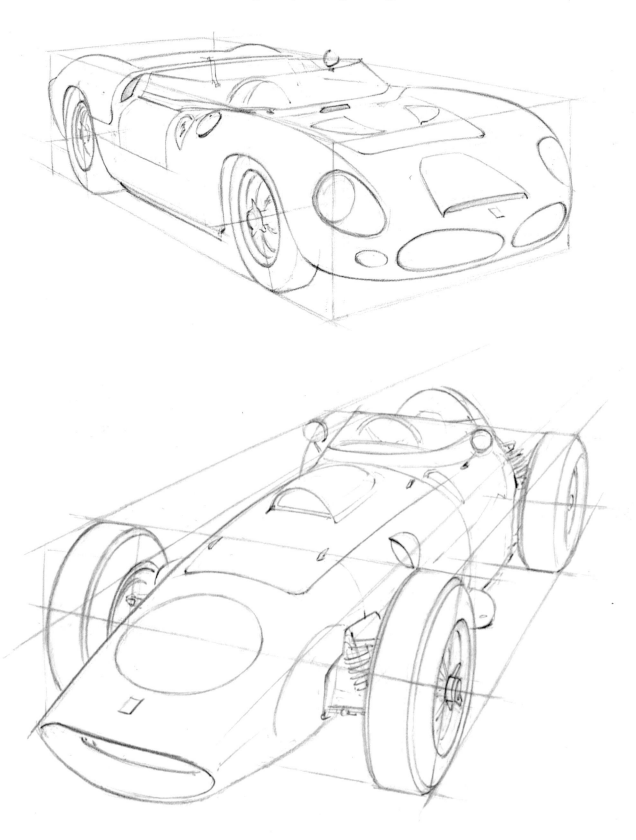

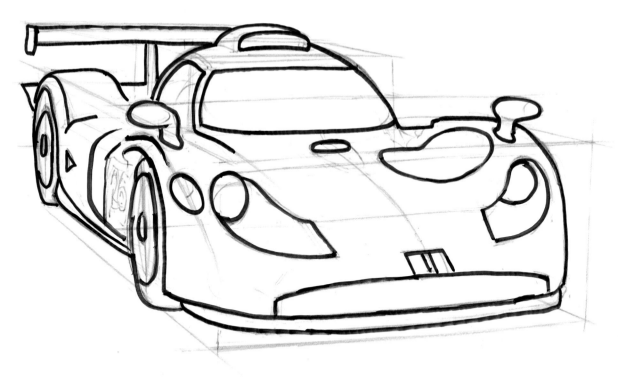

establish or confirm their relationship in your drawing.

Ultimately, this is an important test to pass, and to throw another ingredient in when you thought it wasn't so difficult after all, it is sometimes advantageous to exaggerate or emphasize a particular feature or characteristic of a car to enhance the impression, but don't overdo this or you may stray into the realms of caricature.

Chapter Five

Curved surfaces

Cars in any shape or form are often clothed in a complex blend of curved panels, and to understand the drawing of vehicles in three-dimensional form the best starting point is to study a specific shape from side-on, and then notice how it changes as you move around it. Any car will do for this exercise, so if you have one handy go and see for yourself. Panels which curve away from your line of sight diminish in relation to closer masses which become more dominant, and you will lose sight of some characteristic features totally if you select a viewpoint which denies their visual presence. There are ways of defining these aspects of a three-dimensional interpretation, and on the following pages there are illustrations which will perhaps help you to

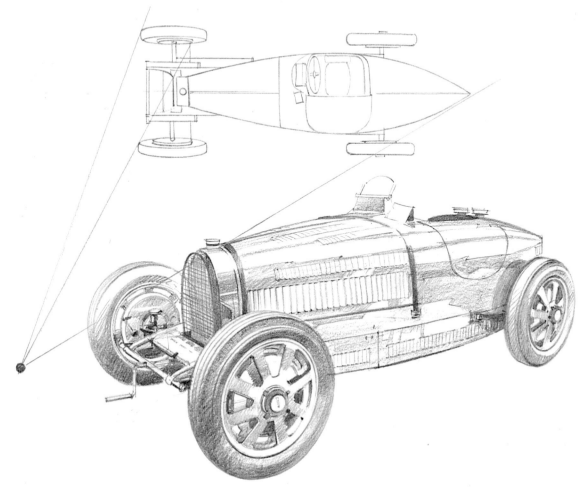

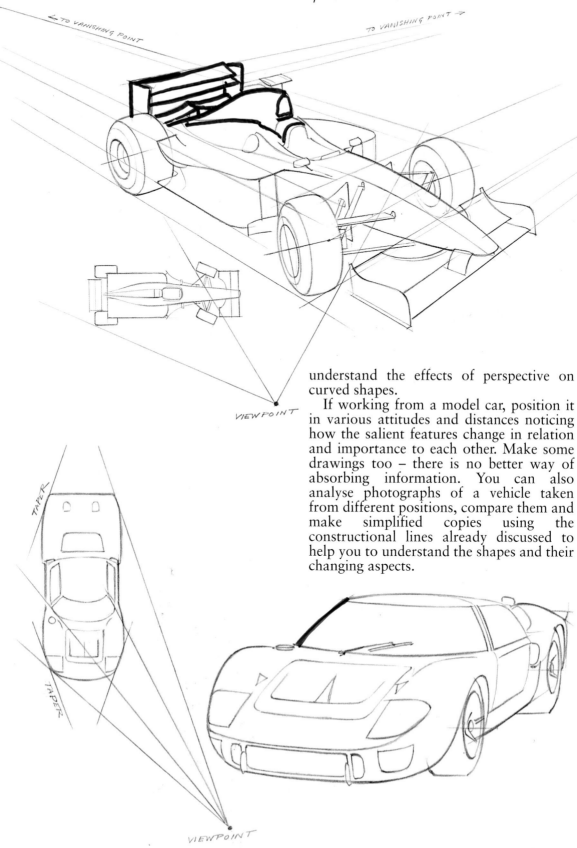

understand the effects of perspective on curved shapes.

If working from a model car, position it in various attitudes and distances noticing how the salient features change in relation and importance to each other. Make some drawings too – there is no better way of absorbing information. You can also analyse photographs of a vehicle taken from different positions, compare them and make simplified copies using the constructional lines already discussed to help you to understand the shapes and their changing aspects.

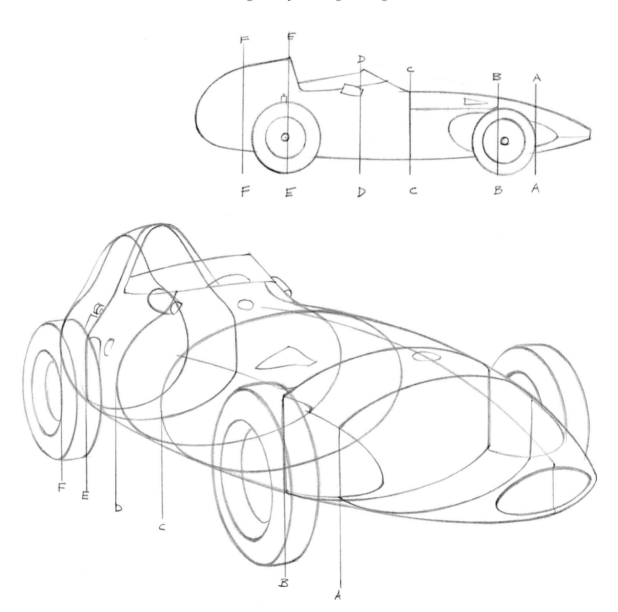

You will probably discover that the more aesthetically pleasing the shape of any object, the more difficult it is to get it right, because a combination of small but subtle shapes and double curvatures all influence the overall appearance but are difficult to pinpoint. Your eye will again have to become the best judge, but this facility usually takes time to develop, and perceptions vary from person to person.

When dealing with complex shapes, particularly the double curvatures just mentioned, it can be useful to sectionalise a vehicle body by introducing formers or templates like the ones used when building model cars (or real ones come to that). These represent the cross section of the shape at a given point, as if sliced through with a knife. Place the sections at chosen intervals along the structure, remembering the effect of perspective, and you can check whether you have the shape right at pertinent points, as in a simple cutaway.

Another problem related to curved panels is the placing of numbers, decals or lettering and making them look as if they conform to the shape on which they are displayed. The modern racing or sports car can present a nightmare, covered as it is with a profusion of advertising motifs and slogans. Simplify the task by imagining each drawn out on a flat surface (as in the case of the individual decal before application), and apply it to the curved panel on your drawing as if actually sticking it down. You can then place the appropriate lettering or design within these guidelines. This method works particularly well when applying the circles upon which racing numbers appear. First draw a square panel on the curved surface, which often bends in two directions, divide it into four quarters by joining the mid-points and

construct your circle. This is not an ellipse because it is not a flat circle, so the segments will not be curved equally. When you have the shape looking right, add the numerals to fill the space, using the divisions to assist their alignment and position within the circle.

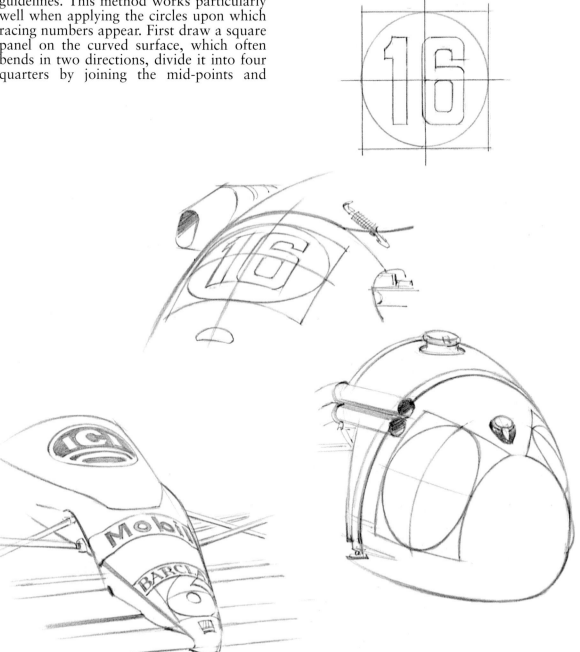

Chapter Six

Light and shade

The way we see things is dependent on light and shade, which in varying degrees give three dimensional form to solid objects and establishes them in space relative to distance. Without light, we can see nothing but darkness, and in low lighting conditions it is difficult to make out objects and judge their size and position.

In daylight, we can easily observe objects and their relationship to each other because of the light falling on them and the shadows cast, which help to define their shape and size. Bright sunlight or strong light sources, either natural or artificial, create stronger shadows than overcast or low light sources. When drawing objects in isolation with no background tones, we outline the outer edges to define their shape because we are not using tone variation to establish the boundaries of these shapes. We should therefore use such lines with restraint and avoid 'outlining' the subject heavily with no consideration of form as, in reality, there is no outline around anything, and we only see shapes because the light which falls on and around them creates contrast with their surroundings.

The length of shadow cast by an object is determined by the direction from which the light is striking it, and the intensity of any such shadow varies according to the strength of this light and the effect of alternative light sources. The sun, in the majority of cases the major light source, is so far away that the rays are parallel, and it is relatively easy to establish the extent and direction of the projected shadow. Artificial light, being much closer, will cast shadows radiating from its location. In the same way that a simple box shape is easier to draw than a complex assembly of curves, so the shadows cast by angular shapes are easier to define than those cast by the complicated contours of objects such as cars. However, as long as you get an

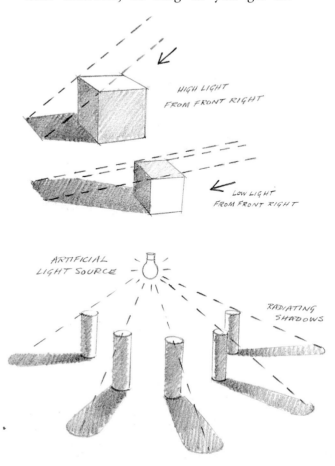

approximation of the shape of the shadow, the direction it is cast in is far more important, and when the object is a moving one the actual shape matters less than if it is stationary.

Once you have placed your primary subject, you should establish your preferred light source, (the direction from which the strongest light is coming), and its intensity. In outdoor scenes, this will normally be the sun, even on an overcast day. However, as we have discovered several times already, life for the artist is rarely simple, and there are usually secondary light sources to consider. These can be from reflected light, i.e. from a nearby surface such as a wall, adjacent ground, water, etc., or from a secondary, perhaps artificial, source. Shiny surfaces such as a car's bodywork can be particularly receptive to reflected light, and this can be used to advantage. For instance, the shadow extending down the unlit side of a car can be relieved by light falling on the adjacent ground and reflecting into it. This is particularly apparent if the bodywork is curved inwards towards the lower edge, as is often the case, helping to convey the shape of the panels and give life and form to an otherwise dull area.

It is worth noting that shadows appear to be darker where they meet adjacent lit areas, and awareness of this effect can be used to heighten the impression of strong images.

When placing objects at varying distances from the viewer, it is vital to remember that we are surrounded by atmosphere, and that as it becomes more dense as we look further and further into the distance, the contrast between tones will reduce, and the shadows will become lighter. The effect of atmosphere on what

REFLECTED LIGHT

REFLECTED LIGHT

1958 Belgian Grand Prix – Tony Brooks's winning Vanwall lines up for the kink on the long Masta Straight. Tonal recession is very apparent on this hot and hazy summer day.

we see is to reduce the contrast between the light and shade as distance increases. Shadows under a car in the foreground will always be darker than those under a car further away, the particles in the air creating a transparent curtain through which we look. The density of the atmosphere can of course vary from hour to hour, day to day, season to season, and this can have an important bearing on the impression you wish to create. Heat haze on a hot summer's day will make distant objects indistinct, but the passage of a weather front, especially in the colder months of the year, can give rise to crystal clarity over great distances, making even far-off objects stand out in sharp contrast. Recession in tonal values is another important ingredient in the conveyance of three-dimensional illusions, and, as we will see later, can also be used to advantage in helping create a sense of movement.

1966 Monaco Grand Prix. Newcomer to the BRM team, Jackie Stewart, storms downhill out of Casino Square on his winning way.

Strong sunlight provides some striking contrasts between open and tree-shaded flashes of the Casino gardens in the background. The light source is coming from behind the car, and the bright highlighted rear bodywork emphasizes this fact. The contrasting dark reflections help to create the three-dimensional illusion. This picture also provides a good example of reflected light, with the sunlit track reflected up into the curved lower bodywork of the car. The long shadows cast forward from the wheels and body conform to the angle of the sun, and help to convey the motion of the car. This is sliding slightly as it reacts to the transformation from lightness over the brow it has just crested, to settling rapidly against the suspension as it accelerates downhill to the Mirabeau Corner.

Dusk at Le Mans, 1964. The Gurney/Bondurant Shelby-Cobra brakes hard for Mulsanne Corner.

A dark car against a dark background of trees – not a great idea in principle, but with the help of some dramatic available light, the scene can come alive. The low light of the setting sun striking the metallic side of the car from three-quarter rear illuminates the graceful curves of the Shelby coupe bodywork, highlighting the contrasting dark of the open perspex window. Light reflected from the sky picks out the roof line against the dark blur of the trees behind. Adding a hint of illumination from the headlights in the half-light and the orange glow from red-hot brake discs makes the most of all the available light sources.

The 1956 Monaco Grand Prix, with Stirling Moss chalking up the first of his victories in this classic event with the works 250F Maserati.

Similar in some ways to the Shelby-Cobra painting, except that the light here is coming from three-quarter front and striking the side of the car, picking out the windscreen and driver's helmet. The backdrop is again a simple one, kept in dark tones to contrast with the subject. The foreground shadows are used to lead the eye to the car, and in this case help rather than hinder the movement because the action is across and into, not out of, the picture. A foreground shadow in the picture on the next page would have had the reverse effect and acted as a block to forward motion.

The 1967 Monaco Grand Prix, with Denny Hulme's winning Brabham sliding round the Gasworks Hairpin hounded by Bruce McLaren's little F2 McLaren.

A more traditional use of light and shade here, with the shadow cast by the tree on the left acting as an anchor or pivot pulling the cars tightly round the apex of the corner. The shadow also provides a dark contrast to the highlighted front and windscreen of the lead car. This strong lighting creates correspondingly strong shadows, their shape and direction helping the flow of the movement. Don't forget that shadows cast by the car can also fall on parts of the car itself, evidenced on the rear tyre. The multitude of buildings in the background are also lit in the same way, but being further away the shadow contrasts are much reduced, helping to give the feeling of distance and depth to the scene and allowing the foreground to dominate.

The 1988 Daytona 24 Hours, with Jaguar's winning XJR 9 sweeping round the banking in the stadium.

A night-time picture, which is lit from the grandstand lights behind us, their highlights reflected in the car's bodywork and windscreen. The lights in the pits below provide background illumination, and the headlights of the following Nissan help define the back of the Jaguar, whose progress is further assisted by the directional sweep of its own headlight beams.

The 1960 Tour de France. A tremendous battle developed between the Ferrari 250GT SWBs of Belgian drivers Willy Mairesse and Olivier Gendebien, and reached a climax at the Belgian circuit at Spa, Francorchamps. Here, Mairesse holds a tenuous lead over his compatriot as they exit the Stavelot Curve, pedal to the metal.

Again, strong sunlight to create strong shadows, and plenty of dark tone behind the cars to prevent the eye from straying out of the picture on the right. The tree trunk helps to complete the block, but I am touching on the functions of composition, which will be dealt with later. The use of light and shade does, however, provide a major compositional tool, so the point is not really out of place here. Your light source has to be consistent throughout the picture of course, and you will notice that the house and observers hut are fully compatible with the chosen direction. It should be borne in mind, however, that the direction of light should relate to conditions associated with the time of day and location depicted, as these factors can have a marked effect on credibility. Make the available surroundings and conditions work for you, rather than serve your own convenience by invention.

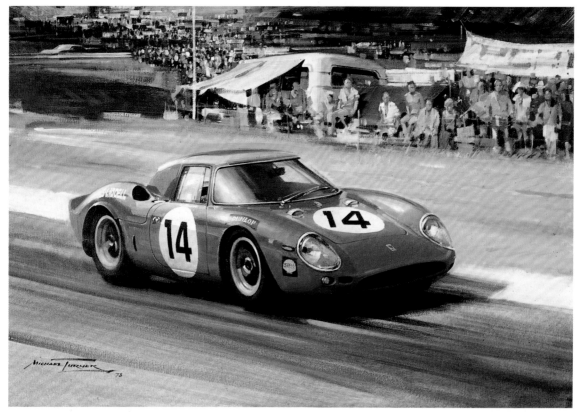

Kyalami, South Africa. The Skailes/Liddell Ferrari 250LM at speed in the evening sun.

The shadows here have been used to aid the composition as well as enhancing the feeling of a hot dry day out in the southern hemisphere. The positioning of the areas of shadow in the background help enormously by following the direction of the movement, giving the car an additional push across the canvas, holding the attention briefly with light falling on the bus and adjacent crowd before moving on.

1991 German Grand Prix, Hockenheim. Andrea de Cesaris urges the emergent Jordan F1 car on to one of the long straights amongst the pine woods.

When faced with a circuit which offers relatively little in the way of inspiring backgrounds, it often leads to an opportunity to show off a more side-on view of a single car than that which one would normally choose. Utilising the availability of an uncomplicated backdrop of dark trees and sunlit track, we can concentrate on the effects created by shadows and reflections to emphasise the sleek shape and attractive colouring of this newcomer to the scene. The slight tilt of the driver's head, and the proximity of the striped kerbing should tell us that the car

has exited a left-hand bend, and is using all the available track as it straightens up for the dash to the next corner.

Pure white is the brightest tone you have in your palette, so reserve it for the brightest light you will need and use it selectively. In strong sunlight, this will be the centre of any highlight catching the sun's rays. Dark reflections of the surrounding trees in the shiny bodywork of the car help to give form and convey the hardness and gloss of its finish.

1970 Targa Florio, with Swiss Jo Siffert hurrying the Gulf team's Porsche 908 Spyder through Collesano on his winning way.

Unlike Hockenheim, the Sicilian classic offers an infinite choice of scenic settings for the artist to exploit. A true road race through hills and villages, with the encouragement of the local population to urge the competitors on their way, and more often than not the ambience of the hot Mediterranean sun to add warmth and colour to the occasion. In this scene, light and shade is used to contrast the buildings with the rather flat and unattractive lines of the winning car, and the shadowy foliage of the overhanging trees and their trunks help to contain the composition by encircling the vehicle.

Night section on the 1955 Tulip Rally – the Gott/O'Hare-Moore AC Ace catches a triumph TR2.

1997 Belgian Grand Prix at Spa. A triumph for the skills of Michael Schumacher, who excelled in the soaking wet conditions of the Ardennes to bring his Ferrari home first. Here he leads the opening laps at Les Combes, the highest part of the circuit, chased by Jean Alesi's Benetton and the Jordan of brother Ralf Schumacher.

One of the most striking and dramatic lighting conditions can occur when heavy rain is suddenly followed by bright sunlight. Here was just such an occasion, presenting for a brief period, strong well-lit colours contrasted against thunderously dark skies. Reflections in the streaming waterlogged track and plumes of spray kicked up behind the slithering cars add to the drama. The normally matt surface of the track is now shiny and darkened in tone, and is reflecting the shapes of the car wheels, with stronger reflections from the front wing and tyre on the inside of the corner where the water is laying more. The

figures at the trackside are wearing waterproofs which are also reflective from their wet surfaces, and the sun shining on the bright red of the Ferrari is creating highlights which assist in indicating the shape of the bodywork. The tyres, much shinier than usual because they are wet, are also catching the glint of the sun and reflecting highlights. In spite of the conditions, the cars are still clean on this opening lap, but if the picture was representing a later stage in the race they would have to look much more grimy and travel-stained.

1989 Monaco Grand Prix. Ayrton Senna takes the McLaren through the swimming pool complex under blue skies towards one of six wins in the Principality.

In contrast to the previous painting, this one shows cars in action in the dry. The road surface does not have that dark slippery reflective surface, and the slick sticky tyres are dull by comparison. There are shadows on the road and a hint of rubber dust coming off the tyres takes the place of the spray in assisting movement. Notice that the white car body is not really white, absorbing the colours that surround it. Remember that even on a white surface, highlights show and therefore the brightest white must be reserved for them. The Armco barriers are made of dull anodised metal, the colours of adjoining sections varying slightly, and the advertising hoardings are made of board. There are plenty of different textures to consider as you paint, and some thought should be given to each as you work on them.

1970 BOAC 1,000km, Brands Hatch. Another drenchingly wet event, with Chris Amon holding a temporary lead round Druids Hairpin from the Porsche 917s of Elford and Rodriguez.

Plenty of reflections here to play with. Mirror images such as this reflect vertically downwards, but the tricky bit is that you are looking at a reflection which shows the underside of the object above it as you look down into it. If you turn the image upside down, you will have a correspondingly low viewpoint of the same vehicle, except that things like numbers and letters are in reverse.

1983 San Marino Grand Prix, Imola. A win for Patrick Tambay's Ferrari, not the prettiest of cars to come out of Maranello, with bathtub seating position and ungainly rear wings sprouting in a very odd looking manner. Nelson Piquet's much more stylish Brabham spoils its looks in the background as it flies off the track in an effort to take the lead at the Aqua Minerale Corner.

The upper surface of the Ferrari sidepods are reflecting the decals from the area above, but, as the race draws to a close, the rest of the bodywork has lost much of its shine, with dust and grime dulling the nose cone and flanks.

The Datsun 240Z of Shekhar Mehta and Lofty Drews hurries on its way to win the 1973 East African Safari Rally.

The dust and mud of Africa have taken the shine off this once pristine Datsun and left it looking pretty travel-stained. Rally cars very rapidly get into various stages of grubbiness at best, with not infrequent additional modifications to their shape as well! Certainly a scene such as this would lose credibility if the car was painted with too many reflections, although the hard surface of the bodywork still needs to be borne in mind.

Jaguar's XJ-13 makes a high-speed test run on the MIRA banking with test driver Norman Dewis at the wheel. The car was never actually raced, so its potential will remain a mystery.

Here we have a nice, clean shiny and smooth sports car with no advertising decals plastered all over it to interrupt the treatment of light and reflections. The car is lit from the right and slightly behind, which gives scope for a good gradation of tone to follow the curving top line of the bodywork. A dark area defines the drop where the nearside front wing joins the bonnet, with a corresponding touch of light on the opposite side. The tone is graded from light to dark across the front of the car to give it shape as the light source gets more oblique to the surface, and the highlights on the sidescreen, body and silver wheels help to give sparkle. The hint of dust kicking up is well behind the car, indicating that it is covering the ground fairly rapidly, while the treetops and the line of the clouds make it clear that the car is on steep banking and not on a flat road which has been tilted to give more impact to the picture.

The then new Jaguar XKSS gets a public airing at Brands Hatch before the main event.

Another nice clean shiny car, and a Jaguar again! The race track is fairly well dominated by advertising hoardings at Bottom Bend, now called Graham Hill Bend, all seemingly striving to be seen amongst their companions but, apart from lending a competitive flavour to the setting, they provide a backdrop which contrasts well with the clean uncluttered lines of the car. Notice that the line of reflection between lighter top surfaces and darker undercurves of the bodywork continue through the headlamp glazing, but with a less distinct variation because of the difference in the reflective qualities of the surfaces. Also, the screen is clear to reveal the occupants, being viewed almost head-on, but the light on the side window is nearly opaque, although you can tell that it too is transparent. The frame of the windscreen is reflected in the bonnet top, but its line is distorted by the bulge in the centre.

Le Mans 1989, with the winning Mercedes-Benz in the pits on Sunday for a routine stop.

After racing for many hours, cars become understandably very grimy, an oily film picked up from the atmosphere to which road dust and hapless insects stick, progressively obscuring the once shiny paintwork. Someone obsessed with company image has obviously wiped the Mercedes motif clean amidst the frantic activity of a brief period at rest, providing visual evidence of how dirty the car has become, and an interesting detail to be recorded. The windscreen has already been cleaned, and reflects the driver installing himself for a spell at the wheel. The treatment of the texture of pit crew and drivers' clothing differs from the hard shine of their helmets, and the overflow container held in place on the right rear of the car has the yellowish hue of discoloured plastic.

1959 Le Mans 24 Hours. A triumph for the Aston Martin driven by Roy Salvadori and Carol Shelby. After a wet night, the very travel-stained DBR1 with Salvadori at the wheel swings through Indianapolis Corner in the lead on Sunday morning.

The early morning sun casts shadows across the track from the trees on the left, used again to help project the foreground subject. The metal bodywork reflects only a dull shine from the sun's rays, coated as it is with dirt and dust, a very different state to that in which it started the race the previous day. The tyre marks following the racing line through the corner were put in after painting the white centre-lines on the road, a logical but planned progression as the painting neared completion.

1985 Brands Hatch 1000kms. The resurgent TWR Jaguar team were getting into their stride, and here the two XJR-6s lead through Stirling's Bend.

Shadows cast by trackside trees create a tonal break between the foreground car and the middle distance, the dull glint of the sun on the windscreen helping to lift the car out of the darker background. Tonal gradation on the big double curvature windscreens of modern sports cars is always a bit of a facer, because you have to achieve both a smooth change of tone across the curve and some hard reflections, at the same time indicating the form of a driver behind the perspex. Decide roughly what you want to achieve, then work as quickly as possible keeping the paint fairly wet, indicate the driver's helmet shape and brush lightly over it to retain the impression that the driver is behind the screen, not painted on it. Don't worry about painting over the edges of the frame, as you can tidy these up later. Difficult enough, but if, as was the fashion at the time, the top of the screen had a band across it carrying the maker's name, with a straight edge also curving with the surface it was stuck to, you could be forgiven for flinging your brushes across the room in frustration! One possible answer to such a problem could be to apply a mask, cut to the required shape from drafting tape, over the already completed screen, and paint up to or across it, matching the tone changes to those of the curved screen, then peeling it off carefully when dry. I have not tried this method yet because I have only just thought of it, but it might be a solution worth considering. Otherwise, it is very much a case of technique developed with practice, and you may like to be forewarned before choosing such cars as your subjects.

Lagonda out for a summer jaunt.

Not exactly a racing car, but an example of the treatment of two adjoining materials of very different appearance. In common with other sports cars of the period, which included the famous racing Bentleys, the rear body from the scuttle backwards was often covered in fabric and painted in the same colour as the bonnet and other metalwork, providing an interesting exercise in observation and painting technique. As an added challenge, the mud protection skirts on the inside of the front wheels were made of leather on this model, the stretched folds giving the clue to a material less rigid than metal.

Monaco in 1932, with Tazio Nuvolari swinging through the Tabac Corner in his winning P2 Alfa Romeo chased by the white-painted Alfa of Carracciola.

Sunshine and shadow creating contrasts against the bleached concrete of the road help to make the car stand out strongly in this composition. The afternoon sun is striking the radiator cowl of the leading Alfa, a yellowish oily patina bestowing a nice warm tint to the dull red of the car. The rubber of the tyres is picking up a sheen, and in the suroundings we have the texture of wooden boards and the patchwork of a rough stone wall. The painted metal bonnet of the car is reflecting blue from the Mediterranean sky and the bodywork has lost its polished shine on forward facing surfaces, telling us that the race has been on for some time. It can be a little tricky blending in blue with red, as it has a tendency to turn purple or mucky, or both, but it is worth persevering to achieve the benefits of the effect.

1968 Dutch Grand Prix, Zandvoort. Jackie Stewart splashes his way to victory in the rain, tip-toeing round the Tarzan Hairpin at the end of the pit straight.

More clear reflections here, and plenty of spray to give movement and direction. The car's windscreen is fairly opaque from rain and dirt, but Jackie's visor is clear enough to allow us to see his facial features. The pale greenish hue of the plastic imparts a rather unhealthy palor to his face. Even those lucky punters in the shelter of the grandstand are pretty damp and cold, a feeling implied by the low scudding rain clouds partly obscuring the seaside town's not so distant tower block. The special hand-cut Dunlop rain tyres have that previously mentioned glossy blackness, resulting from their wet surface.

Chapter Eight

Composition

Composition is probably one of the most important issues to consider when creating a picture, for no matter how well you portray the primary object of your attention, if this is not placed sympathetically in relation to the other elements in the illustration with the overall effect in mind, the result will probably fail to impress. When I first read about composition as an 11-year-old, I was frankly baffled as to the reason for the specific placing of objects to balance larger objects and areas of tone, and the general arrangement of pictorial elements which somehow were supposed to affect the general appeal and impact of a picture. Do not be dismayed – your understanding of composition will either evolve from a natural sense of pictorial balance, in common with one for perspective and proportion, or it can hopefully develop in time with a growing understanding resulting from explanations and advice.

There are formulae designed to help determine the composition of a picture, but I have never had the patience or inclination to examine them in detail. As a general rule for starters, you can draw a horizon line

✔

✗

✗

✗

two thirds of the way up your picture area to represent eye level, and position the main object below and a little off centre, not in the exact middle. The placing of other secondary objects should help to lead the eye through or around the picture in whatever direction you choose, to provide the best emphasis to achieve the desired objective. In other words, unless you want the viewer's attention to wander about aimlessly, place an appropriate item or a tonal block to prevent this happening. If you want to convey movement in any particular direction, as in an action painting of a moving car or cars, try to place items to not only discourage the tendency of the eye to move away from the desired direction, but to positively encourage it to move towards the way out of the picture which follows the movement you want to create.

It is important to provide space for a moving object to progress into, so as a general rule, leave more in front of your racing car than behind it, assuming that it is not going backwards of course. If it is moving across the picture from left to right, then place the car to the left of centre, leaving space on the right for it to move into. Never place the front of a moving object too close to the border of the picture – this will only tend to block any sense of movement. If you have placed your car badly when composing your picture, you must bring yourself to redraw it in a better position or risk wasting even more of your time and efforts on a picture doomed to failure. Having said all that, my 'let-out' clause is that there may of course be reasons to justify some deviation from generally accepted rules. However, we do not need to confuse the issue at this stage with such advanced applications, where one deliberately creates an unbalanced composition to achieve a particular effect or emphasis.

In addition to the thoughtful placing of major and minor objects, choice of lighting, shadows and even cloud or sky formations can be applied to advantage. It is more than useful to spend a little time producing 'thumbnail' sketches, blocking in areas of tone representing both solid objects and tonal shapes until you achieve a

satisfactory balance and can progress to a more fully developed working plan. As inferred by the term, these need only be very small and completely lacking in detail, but you will be surprised how quickly you can appraise various ideas and ways of looking at a subject in this way, with minimum waste of time.

*Thumbnail sketch for
1964 Le Mans painting.*

Some typical thumbnail scribbles, done while thinking up a suitable composition to portray the Hamilton/Rolt D-Type Jaguar at Le Mans in 1954. These quick visuals are a good way of giving one's thoughts an airing as they flit through the mind. Those which are obviously non-starters can be discarded without wasting time on them, and it also makes it easier to select the best of the bunch. This can then be worked up to a more finished state, with the composition more carefully worked out to take account of fixed features, lighting and the relationship between the primary and secondary objects. This is the sort of finish adequate for consideration by a client before commencing the actual painting.

Incidentally, I rarely embark on colour roughs, as I find it very difficult to repeat what are often chance effects created with a single brush stoke on a small scale. In the past, this sometimes led me to a degree of disappointment in the finished work, which failed to achieve the same result in larger scale. There are, of course, times when you will want to check out colour combinations, and many artists do follow this pattern of working, so it ultimately is, as always, a matter of personal choice.

1972 French Grand Prix – Clermont-Ferrand. Jackie Stewart again, this time winning in the Tyrrell-Ford. Jacky Ickx is in hot pursuit on the downhill sweep into the braking area for the corner into the pit straight early in the race.

The positioning of the red Ferrari helps to 'nudge' the back of the Tyrrell to emphasize the sliding inclination of the car on the limit of adhesion, the rear tyres on the point of snapping sideways. The figures on the right behind the Armco act as an anchor, or pivot, as well as providing a bit of interest, looking up the track to watch the approach of the next arrival. The dark shaded tree on the right also provides a useful block to prevent the eye from wandering out of the picture, leading it instead across the background to absorb the scene before tempting it back via the Tannoy speaker on a pole and the yellow board and figure on the earth bank to the main subject again. With careful manipulation and positioning of available features and incidental items in your composition, without blatant distortion of the way things are, it is possible to dictate the priorities and reaction of your audience, and transmit the impression you wish to create.

Can-Am cars in Canada. A poster design for a 1977 event, the space-age appearance of the Schkee seems rather out of keeping with the ageing nature of Mosport's popular and scenic track.

The vertical format was dictated by the requirement for poster artwork, and provision of space at the top right and bottom of the painting was incorporated to accommodate the words announcing the event. However, when this surplus is trimmed away, we still have a composition which conveys speed and excitement. The cars have just burst over the brow, the drivers already aiming for the blind apex of the fast downhill left-hander, and the angle of drift assumed by the two leading cars is emphasized by their relationship to the white line defining the inside of the turn. As with the previous picture, I have positioned the following cars to help throw the leading car off balance, but the slight correction visible on the front wheel and the steadying effect of the straddled white line is keeping things just under control. The trees and figures in the background also guide the eye in a vertical direction downwards, in keeping with the planned movement.

*1951 French Grand Prix – Reims. Luigi Villoresi takes his Ferrari through La Garenne Corner,
leading on to the long straight to Thillois Hairpin on a hot July day.*

The distant view across the hazy summer landscape is held by the strong vertical of the tree trunk, the overhanging foliage preventing the eye from moving straight up and out of the picture, and the white roadsign which, by chance, also serves to establish the location. The more dominant message comes, however, from the horizontal elements of the dark treeline in the middle distance, light sunlit strip of field, dark crowd of spectators, the white line demarking the road and the red car moving across the scene. The driver's head cutting the white line attracts the eye to this important focal point, where the attitude of the driver adds a sense of urgency. The shadowed foreground also helps to push the eye into the action, and the kilometre post, held back by shadow, completes the linking movement. The telegraph poles and distant building to the right add just enough vertical influence to dissuade the eye from following the movement off the edge of the picture completely, without interrupting the flow, unlike the positive block of the tree on the left.

1957 German Grand Prix – Fangio forces his 250F Maserati past Peter Collins's Ferrari, throwing up dirt from the apex of the North Turn under the eye of the Schloss Nürburg, to close relentlessly on Mike Hawthorn in the leading Ferrari.

On page 18 the painting of the same event depicted the two Ferraris being reeled in by Fangio's Maserati, and this picture shows the drama continuing to build at the commencement of the following lap. Such notable events often call for more than one interpretation, and the moment chosen here needed a totally different approach. It was in fact painted many years before the other picture, and I felt at the time it was important to get right in among the action on the track to highlight Fangio's commitment and skill. The rear view became necessary because if I had chosen a frontal view, it would have highlighted Hawthorn and not conveyed the spirit of the chase with quite the same emphasis. Collins, taken a bit by surprise by Fangio's move, has been put off-balance into an opposite-lock slide, the fact that one of the lenses in his goggles was hit by a stone thrown up from the edge of the track by the Maserati's rear wheel adding to his discomposure. From a compositional perspective, this view also allowed the famous castle to fulfil a role and establish the setting while the marshals' hut and bridge parapet lead the eye progressively in the direction the competing trio is heading towards.

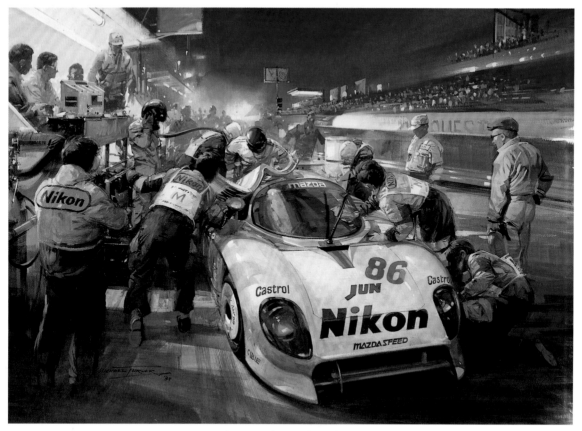

Le Mans 1983 – a pit stop for Mazda on their first visit to the 24-hour classic.

The grouping of the figures and placing of the headlight glare from passing cars in the background help to concentrate the attention on the activity surrounding the driver change-over. The back-lit figures on the pit counter act as a lead-in from the left, and the less conspicuous figures at the right prevent the eye from straying out of the picture. The urgency of the movement in the central figures is heightened by the apparent calm of those not actively involved, and you will notice that the perspective lines in the background, the pit structure and the angle of the car together with the attitudes of the people all converge on the focal point.

Italian Grand Prix – Monza 1988. A rare error by Ayrton Senna, whose McLaren is beached on the kerbing of the chicane, allows Berger and Alboreto to assume the lead for a Ferrari 1–2 on their home ground.

Here is another painting where the composition is influenced by the story to be told, and this view of the tight turns in the first chicane facilitates the positioning of the three cars in a compact area. The instantly recognisable Monza score-tower and the adjacent mass of trees acts as a vertical influence down through the main subject. The introduction of some sunlit foliage on the right draws enough attention to the cameo of the track-workers' efforts to remove the abandoned McLaren, and Senna's exasperated exit from the scene as he removes his helmet. The space to the left is kept low-key, but contains evidence of the pit area and the following group of cars to give depth and secondary interest.

Chapter Nine

Speed, movement and atmosphere

Now that we have the abilities to construct a three-dimensional representation of a racing car and place it in an appropriate composition, we need to breathe life into it. A machine such as a racing car is an inanimate object until the human element is added, and while it is a perfectly satisfactory artistic objective to draw and paint a racing car at rest, concentrating on the challenges of conveying such interesting shapes and textures, lighting and effects, it is from the excitement and drama of speed and competition for which it was intended, that we should get maximum satisfaction.

Raymond Mays's ERA sets a record at Shelsley Walsh Hill-climb.

Duel under the Members' Bridge at Brooklands.

There are many ways of portraying speed and movement in paintings and drawings, and any or all may be employed to make the most appropriate expression of this most stimulating manifestation. If you take a moment to consider what you see when watching a speeding car from a stationary position, you will know that if you follow it with your eyes, the background becomes more or less blurred depending on the speed of travel. If you concentrate your gaze on the background as the car passes, you will see the car as a blur even if it is travelling slowly. We cannot concentrate on both things at the same time. In a painting, however, the viewer can study the whole at his leisure, and in time the extreme blur, whether subject or background, will fail to hold the attention, just as the fleeting impression in reality is exciting because of its transience. Because historically and pictorially I believe it is important to encapsulate both the excitement of movement and the surroundings in which they take place, I personally favour a compromise solution. This means that, while concentrating on the subject and creating an accurate representation of the machine because it is important to me, it is necessary to indicate sufficient information in the surroundings to enable the picture to convey a factual setting. This will serve to hold the interest of the viewer before returning to the overall impression. The relative movement between the vehicle and its surroundings can be indicated by a selective blurring of both, but because the car is the most important element, the principle parts which lend themselves to this treatment are the wheels. Most of the movement can be concentrated on the ground or track over which they are travelling, and the immediate surroundings.

The simple expedient of streaking the road surface is certainly a factor to be considered, but it is a mistake to think that this alone will convey movement in a satisfactory way. When it is overdone, as it often is, you can end up with a comic-book result, and this is not to my mind artistically acceptable if the work is to be

taken seriously. By all means use speed lines to a degree to establish a direction of movement, but do not let them dominate the overall impression by attracting too much attention. Skilful composition of your picture will do more to create a sense of movement than any number of speed lines will ever do, so we must consider how best we can employ the tricks of positioning our major and minor objects, lighting and shadows. Where appropriate, make the most of the presence of rain, cloud, snow, dust, exhaust fumes, rubber dust, etc. The degree of movement must also be considered when composing your picture. When the principal line of action is, as is usually the case, diagonally across your picture, the positioning of verticals, such as buildings, telegraph poles, or background features, can be used to slow down or contain the sense of speed to a greater or lesser extent.

Nuvolari wrestles his Auto Union around the Nürburgring.

1978 German Grand Prix – Hockenheim. Emerson Fittipaldi's Copersucar outbrakes Pironi's Tyrrell into the stadium.

The fairly straightforward use of a blurred background to give movement to a car or cars passing across the picture in the same way that a camera would record the situation if using a slow shutter speed while panning.

Below we see the same exercise as that above, but with the additional benefit of spray from the rain-soaked track. The stormy sky has been used to accentuate the spray behind the car, but relieving the darkness of tone with some light on the horizon to the right has helped to boot the car across the picture. In each case there is a hint of interest in the background without causing a distraction.

1992 French Grand Prix – Magny Cours. Mika Hakkinen's Lotus at speed in the wet.

1984 United States Grand Prix – Detroit. Nelson Piquet's Brabham is challenged in the closing laps by Martin Brundle's sick-sounding Tyrrell, whose detached exhaust didn't help his nonetheless spirited chase.

The sense of movement and excitement are combined at this tight section of the circuit, where the downhill exit from the corner helps to place the cars in this way. The sliding attitude of the Brabham, plus the tilt of Piquet's head, follow through from the angle and lighting on the nose of the Tyrrell threatening from above, and with the photographers acting as a pivot, the composition of the picture plays a dominant role in creating movement. The track marshals, spectators in the bleachers and TV camera stand all have a part to play, with some restrained speed streaks on the track and a puff of dust from the rear wheels thrown in for good measure, but not of prime importance here.

Prince Bira heads the field in his ERA 'Hanuman' at a pre-war Donington Park race meeting.

A simple example of how the positioning of cars can in itself instill a feeling of movement. The leading car is filling the available space, with the wheels quite close to the border of the picture. However, as the thrust of the movement is downwards more than across, this is not as important as in most compositions. There is, nevertheless, more space in front of the car than at the back, in accordance with the general rule. The cars are, as before, placed so that they create a sense of imbalance as they slide towards the apex of the corner in a long, sweeping curve. The contact point between Bira's head and the following car establish this as the focal point, where the movement is pivotal. The use of brush strokes to further direct the motion and atmosphere is very clear in this work, and the shafts of sunlight between the trees also provide a little extra help.

1958 Moroccan Grand Prix, Casablanca. Mike Hawthorn finished second in his Ferrari to clinch the World Championship, and is seen here sweeping through a series of fast bends under the hot North African sun.

The movement here is also basically vertical, but there is less sliding action involved. A combination of suspension movement, body roll, head angle and haze from tyres and exhaust, plus a puff of disturbed sand are important ingredients, and the flowing line of the track diminishing into the distance indicate the speed and relative smoothness of the action. The white lines down the middle of the track establish the angle of drift of the car, and the driver's head cutting the track edge draws the eye to this spot as the desired focal point.

1971 Monaco Grand Prix – Jackie Stewart holds a wild slide coming out of Casino Square with Jacky Ickx hot on his heels.

The track here combines a change of camber and a drop downhill at the very point where adhesion is at a premium. This fact is made apparent from the upward looking view of the buildings and the car in the background, as well as the looking down view of the foreground car and track. The angle of the car to the direction of travel is inferred by the use of the directional streaks on the road surface, which follow the line of rubber put down by the constant passage of tyres. The angle at which the rear wing of the Tyrrell cuts the horizon also helps to create an unbalance and focal point, with the odd shape of the Armco barriers and the grandstand structure contributing to the motion. Their lines tapering with perspective to form that fundamental V-shape again, lead us to the focal point. Although the car image is sharp, the tyres and rear surface of the wing are blurred.

When a racing car negotiates a corner it is subjected in varying degrees to the effects of gravity. The stresses and strains of this energy are concentrated through the tyres (normally the only points of contact between vehicle and terrafirma), and suspension, which try to resist the tendency for the car to succumb to the forces of gravity and run off-course. When painting your action scene, you must therefore try to convey this stress and movement, and observation and study of photographs will help you to interpret these phenomena. As already mentioned, if you can immerse yourself emotionally in the subject as you work, you will find it easier to incorporate 'feel' and the essential sense of excitement we get from seeing cars balanced on the knife-edge of adhesion. The placing of the subject relative not only to the part of the track it is on, but also where it has just come from and where it is going to, will all help the implied movement.

Jacky Ickx in action in a F2 Matra.

Le Mans 1924 – the year of Bentley's first triumph in the 24-hour classic, with the winning 3-litre car driven by Duff and Clement rounding the hairpin in Pontlieue on the old circuit.

The clinically clean custom-built circuits of today allow far less scope for conveying motion than those dusty, stony everyday roads did in the early years of the motorcar and racing. This portrayal of a thundering man-sized heavyweight machine being hauled round a rutted and stone-strewn corner gives ample opportunity to make the most of churned-up dust, flying stones and judder-inferring brush strokes to add urgency and movement. The shadowed solid area and strong kerbstones on the left help pull the car round the corner, while the lesser influence of the straight lines feeding out to the right try to encourage lateral escape from the desired course. The varied use of directional brush strokes are apparent here, their prominence appropriate to the period and nature of machine and environment. The driver, again the focal point, is picked out by using a dark tone in the background behind his white helmet.

You will know from your own experience in a car how even fairly low cornering forces cause the driver to lean into a bend. The action of turning the steering wheel induces shoulder and head inclination, and the angle of a racing driver's body and head should be compatible with the movement of the cars in your picture. When drivers were more visible, their attitudes and actions were very much a part of the implied action, adding excitement and character to the impression and allowing identification of their personalities. Their progressive disappearance into the cocoon of their safety capsules now allows only a glimpse of an all-enclosing helmet and perhaps the top of a gloved hand, but it is still just possible to identify the characteristic attitudes of individual driver's head angles if your observation is acute. Apart from considering aspects such as this, together with composition, I always try to become part of what I am painting, calling on my knowledge and emotions to dictate the manner of my brush strokes.

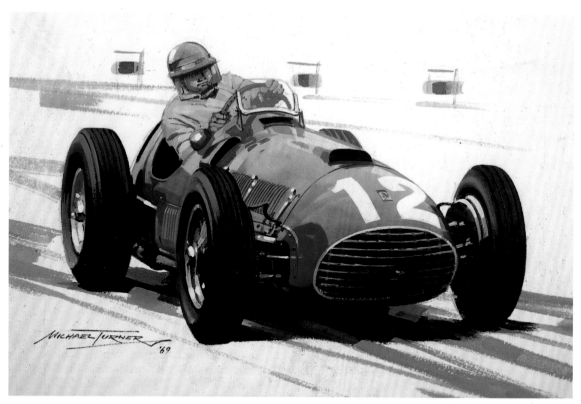

Body weight countering the forces of gravity, brawny arms working overtime to keep the big Ferrari more or less under control, Froilan Gonzales heads for a notable victory at Silverstone.

This is a book illustration, and not intended to be a conventional squared-off painting, but it shows how much easier it is to use the actions of a driver to complement the action when they are visible.

1973 British Grand Prix – Silverstone. A fighting finish to a race which had a sensational start. Peter Revson scored a popular victory in the Yardley-McLaren, with Ronnie Peterson's JPS Lotus, team-mate Denny Hulme's McLaren and James Hunt's Hesketh snapping at his heels across the line.

The drifting, sliding attitudes of the following cars are helped in their movement across the middle of the picture by the widening perspective of the grandstands and earth bank. The vertical influence of the Dunlop tower leads down through the Lotus to bring the action forward with the leading car. The pitched roof of the timekeeper's box on the left points our attention to the chequered flag, and the speed-streaks on the track direct and emphasize the forward movement. As a matter of interest, this is one of the few pictures in which I have used mixed-media, albeit to a very minor extent, by applying chalk over the gouache to the track in the foreground.

When blending your subject car into its surroundings, soften off the tops and rear edges of the tyres and wheels, any moving suspension parts, drive shafts, and generally speaking, the rear surfaces of the bodywork. In modern Formula One racing, high speeds often generate vortices from aerodynamic surfaces such as rear wings, particularly in damp or wet conditions – a bonus for the artist in his quest for ways of imparting movement, just as the use of spray from a wet track thrown up from the speeding wheels can be employed. You would be amazed at the amount of rubber dust and particles that are shed from tyres under stress, and using brush or pencil strokes which suggest this, should be considered. Objects closest to the speeding car will be subject to the most blurring, so as you put in your background remember that the further away things are, the less they will be blurred. It is however important not to define background detail too much, for although recognisable features such as particular buildings, trees, trackside artifacts or distant landscape can all have a part to play, they should never be allowed to distract from the main impression or they will serve only to arrest the sense of movement.

The 1989 Brazilian Grand Prix at Rio. Nigel Mansell scores for Ferrari, taking the lead from Alain Prost's McLaren at the top of the return straight.

In spite of its exotic location, there is really only one choice background at the Jacarapagua circuit, so it was fortunate that the decisive overtaking manoeuvre of the race occurred at this spot. The humid atmosphere was conducive to those vortices from the rear wings, but while they are an additional feature to aid the impression of speed, it would be easy to make them too obvious. The background here is loosely handled, enough to be an interesting piece of scenery but not carrying unnecessary detail to be a distraction.

I mentioned in the chapter on light and shade the importance of tonal recession in creating an impression of depth. Attention to this can also help to give life and movement to your pictures by establishing space between the impact of your foreground object and the lesser tones in the middle distance and background. The darkest tones and greatest contrast will be concentrated in the objects closest to you, the darks becoming progressively lighter as the density of the intervening atmosphere increases with distance.

When creating your composition, the relationship of tonal areas to each other can help to create movement by exaggerating or enhancing the importance of selected elements within the picture. Shadows cast across a track can be used to advantage in this respect, but be careful how you place them. If your car is coming towards you, place the shadow behind it, so that it can burst out towards you. The same shadow placed across the foreground will conversely tend to act as a frame and restrict forward movement. Foreground shadows are largely of use when you want to lead the eye into a more static scene and hold it there. Aim to anchor your composition towards the rear of the subject, giving the eye something to move away from by introducing a point of secondary interest, or a contrasting tone.

Hockenheim and the 1978 German Grand Prix again – this time the Arrows of Stommelen and Patrese negotiate the first chicane.

Not much of a distant view, but the strong shadows behind the leading car are very useful in providing a contrast to the gold paint scheme and a noticeable tone change between the foreground and distant trees.

The tone values on the second car fall in between the two, forming a progression which helps propel the leading car out towards us.

The two major elements missing from any painting are sound and smell, both very pertinent in the sensual perception of motorsport, but if you are successful in the creation of your visual image, these missing senses will be transmitted to the subconscious of the viewer by implication.

While considering the interpretation of speed and movement, we should therefore also think about atmosphere. This can itself have a considerable bearing on the outcome and effectiveness of your painting, as it embraces the unseen constituent, the disturbance of the air surrounding your moving object.

In visual terms, there is nothing much tangible to record, but in emotional terms we should try to convey these reactions to the senses by the way we interpret and manipulate the paint or medium. This can be done by feeling the way the brush, pencil, or whatever you are using to produce a visual image, is applied to the surface upon which you are working. All very esoteric, but it can have a profound effect in communicating your impressions to the viewer. The more visible signs of atmosphere there are in the overall surroundings the better, because you can use rain, mist, fog, dust, humidity, heat haze, and the surrounding conditions to your advantage.

1961 Monaco Grand Prix – Stirling Moss and Phil Hill negotiate Station Hairpin.

Speed, movement and atmosphere

When it comes to the less apparent atmospheric disturbances, then the direction and subtlety of brush strokes can create the impression of movement by disturbing the appearance of background and colour to a greater or lesser extent. Do not overdo this by exaggerating the effects too much, but used sympathetically such techniques can enhance a feeling of vitality and life into an otherwise static impression. Think about the exhaust noise as well as the almost invisible fumes, the tyre noise as well as the presence of rubber dust, the disturbed air surrounding the moving car, the heat from the hot engine and the vibrant stresses and energy of the machine and the driver. All this excitement should be radiated and reflected in the surroundings, be they inanimate scenery or motivated spectators. If it helps, and you don't mind the risk of being taken away to the funny farm, perhaps you could consider making appropriate noises or playing suitable sound effects when you are working, but total immersion in the scene you are portraying should be sufficient if you have a strong enough imagination. The extent of your commitment and enthusiasm will surely enhance the result.

If you can work quickly, so much the better, because initial excitement in your subject will inevitably dissipate proportionately over the length of time you are involved in the painting process, in turn affected by your personal emotional limitations. If you become over interested in a particular segment of your picture, you must try to regenerate your initial enthusiasm to an increasing degree, or risk getting bogged down and losing this elusive ingredient called atmosphere.

A foggy day on the Tulip Rally, with John Gott slithering his way through the murk and mud in his works Sunbeam Tiger, headlights reflecting in the puddles to liven up the foreground.

1972 Monte-Carlo Rally. Sandro Munari slides the winning Lancia through the spectator-packed crest at La Turbie on hard-packed snow, lit by the floodlights of the television cameras.

Snow isn't a factor in circuit racing, but in rallying it offers equal scope with the elements of rain and dust for exploitation in the visual portrayal of speed. The contrasting areas of bright light and shadow are positioned to assist the progress of the action, combined with the clouds of powdered snow and ridges in the foreground. The strong shadow break between headlights and bank form a more static focal point which increases the swinging motion of the rear of the car. The contradictory directional lines in the snow beyond the car and the puff of snow behind the nose of the car suggest the rather more unexpected directional changes inherent in rallying compared with circuit racing.

1953 Italian Grand Prix – Monza. After a race-long battle, the struggle for victory became frantic, and Alberto Ascari's Ferrari overdid it going into the Parabolica for the last time. Farina took avoiding action and spun off, and the wily Fangio slashed past a preoccupied Marimon on the inside to take the win for Maserati.

A situation which can call for a number of rough thumbnails to explore the various ways of looking at an incident before arriving at the best solution. In this case, Ascari's error was the catalyst, so it is logical that the picture should have him as the main feature. To have his car facing the wrong way would both establish the fact that his car was spinning, and allow the other three players to be seen in their relative positions and indicate what was about to unfold. The strong sweeping line of the tail of the foreground car combined with the positions of the other cars lead the eye to Ascari and his efforts to control his wayward machine. Farina has clipped the trackside tyre markers, sending one flying, and is about to lose control, and Marimon's front wheels are locked, tyres smoking under heavy braking. Fangio is best placed to size-up the situation, and is poised to take his opportunity down the inside.

1970 Le Mans 24 Hours. Dickie Attwood swings into the Esses on a wet Sunday morning in the Porsche 917 he shared with Hans Herrmann to score the first of many wins in the event for the marque.

Another device for creating a sense of movement in a picture is by setting up an interplay between focal points of different importance. After initial attraction to the main subject, the eye here is mildly attracted to the bridge on the horizon, with the assistance of the right-hand trackside bank. However, the stronger influence of the tree line on the left and the perspective of the track draw the eye back via the following car. That the eye is encouraged to travel between these two points in a controlled way enhances the impression of movement.

1968 Dutch Grand Prix – Zandvoort. Side by side round the Tarzan Corner, wheels interlocking and almost touching, the Lotuses of Graham Hill and Jo Siffert vie for the lead.

This type of action demands close involvement, and the viewpoint chosen combines close proximity to the opponents, and the more expansive view of the surrounding background to maximize the excitement of the contest. The blurred figure of the photographer forms a link with the grandstand, the eye then following the secondary cars back round to the main subject in a circular motion.

Chapter Ten

Backgrounds

I have mentioned backgrounds in the previous chapter as a contributory factor to the overall impression of movement. We also need to give some thought to the matter in its own right however, because a well drawn or painted racing car will cease to be convincing if it is placed in a poorly executed setting.

My early attempts at drawing cars and aeroplanes were confined largely to my interest in the machines themselves, but in order to do justice to the reason for their existence it became necessary to indicate at least some elements of their surrounding environment. One of the first lessons I learned, before I even got to art school, was that if I was to do anything half worthwhile in artistic terms with what talent I possessed, I would have to direct my attention to other things in everyday life. My instinctive understanding for perspective and form, and the ability to use my imagination for the interpretation of dramatic occurrences, would count for nothing if I was unable to produce convincingly constructed surroundings for my speeding machines. This was quite a hurdle for me to overcome, because it meant spending seemingly valuable time away from the objects of my obsession. Trees and buildings, skies and landscape and, most difficult of all, the human figure, demanded a concentrated effort on my part. Fortunately I discovered that the extent of one's perseverance is measured by the strength of one's ambition and purpose and I found that all these areas were artistically challenging in their own right, and fascinating enough to bring their own satisfaction. That was sound fundamental advice, and if you have to sweat blood it is well worth the effort to provide an all round competence to complement rather than let down your interest in machines.

If you have the ability to produce a satisfactory drawing of a racing car, then you have the ability to do the same with other three-dimensional objects. The extensive study of other subjects is not however in the remit of this book, and I won't attempt to take up the much wider subject of general drawing and painting, but there are plenty of books which do, and I recommend that you spend some time at least looking at things around you and stimulating an understanding which can only enhance the quality of your work. As with the drawing of the racing car, the many other objects which will come into your pictures will be more convincing if you feel their form as you work. A tree trunk is a very solid thing for instance, so think about it and the space around and behind it if there is one in your chosen setting. Likewise with buildings, be they simple or complex structures, think about their construction and solidity. You don't have to be a botanist or an architect to discern their appearance and form.

It is important to consider incorporating interesting backgrounds not only to locate the event depicted and increase the viewer's interest, but to use them to advantage in your compositions. Regrettably, modern custom-built race tracks cannot provide as much variety and interest in their settings as the circuits of more historic events, but if you look hard enough, there are still features to be found which provide artistic scope. Unfortunately, magazine photographers are often unable to get to positions which afford much background pictorial coverage, resorting to long-focal lenses to capture detailed shots of the competing cars to the exclusion of the surroundings, so such references can be limiting in this respect. A good alternative is to study video coverage and try to build up a choice of settings to complement your racing car references. Attendance at an event should by a priority and, if you are able to visit various tracks, it is very worthwhile to get around on occasions

other than practice and race days, when mobility is easier, to collect references of as many useful scenes as possible for future background use. You will be better served for pictorial reference if your interests are from past eras, but whatever your preference it is well worthwhile spending time on this aspect as it is sure to help you produce more convincing pictures.

1978 South African Grand Prix, Kyalami. Ronnie Peterson's JPS Lotus snatches the lead from Patrick Depailler's Tyrrell on the last lap.

The grandstands and control towers of the start-finish area, with spectators thronging the grassy banks overlooking Clubhouse Bend, form an interesting and vibrant backdrop to this scene. The strong perspective of the track leads straight out of this centre of interest, and it is useful if

you can incorporate interesting snippets which also fit conveniently into the composition. In this instance the abandoned Arrows of Patrese, who led the race for many laps until his engine expired, fills a space which would otherwise allow the eye to wander out to the right.

1974 Spanish Grand Prix, Jarama. Rain again, this time in Spain and on the plain. Niki Lauda and Clay Reggazoni win for Ferrari.

Exiting a slippery uphill left-hander, the spot allows an interesting view of the impressive control tower and the start-finish area and pits below. The use of directional lines on the track, plus the corrective steering applied, indicate the sliding progress of the Ferrari. The perspective lines of the grandstands and roofs in the background help with the directional movement, while the strong vertical position of the tower imparts a steadying vertical influence. The eye-level is quite high, giving a distant horizon, but the gradient of the track in the foreground dictates a lower vanishing point, allowing a useful combination of panoramic scenery and close action.

1956 Mille Miglia. Eugenio Castellotti's Ferrari sweeps through a rain-swept town on its winning way.

This is another example of action encouraged by eye movement between minor and major focal points. As in the Le Mans painting on page 98, the eye is led to the distant brow, in this case by the vertical confines of the buildings lining the road, joined by the banner stretched between them. A progression in tone strength via the car in the middle distance to the archways and figure group on the left brings us to the major focal point, the Ferrari, as it swings across the picture in front of us. The spray and streaked reflections of the headlights in the wet road speed up the movement, and the figures on the right, although not disturbing the motion of the car, provide the link back up the street again.

1992 Belgian Grand Prix – Spa. Michael Schumacher wins his first grand prix in the Benetton-Ford, hurtling into the daunting Eau Rouge Corner chased by team-mate Martin Brundle.

An instantly recognisable view of the old pits, used in conjunction with a dramatic head-on view of the car. The composition is designed to concentrate on the rapid movement, with the track leading in from top right to the area directly behind the car, the point where the right-hand verge meets the rear wing of the car and providing a link to the focal point. The eye is temporarily diverted from continuing across the picture by the kink and Armco on the left, and is then re-directed via the car straight towards the viewpoint. There are other minor participants in the plot, the tower leading in from the top of the picture directly above the car for instance, while you will find other directional leads, such as the use of that trusty V-shape formed by the tree line at the top, repeated by the grandstand roof.

1948 RAC Grand Prix – Silverstone. The start of the first event at the disused wartime airfield which grew into the sophisticated modern circuit we now know.

There are times when the setting takes precedence over the participants, without diminishing the competitive atmosphere of the content. The start of an event presents such a possibility, but it is probably more conventional to show such moments from the front of the field. However, when I turned up a contemporary photograph taken from the top of a bridge over the track, I found the scene so fascinating that it formed the basis for this picture in spite of the fact that the field would have to be viewed from behind. Perspective again plays an important part by introducing movement and direction to a wide panoramic scene, and the placing of the cars, while factual, is designed to help the feeling of movement by adding to the tonal recession. Such scenes often lead to long periods of research, for the information from one reference is rarely clear enough in all areas. What happens behind the pits, for instance. Is there a fence? What colour was the tarpaulin roofing? What is written on the scoreboard? Colour photographs from early periods are rare if not totally non-existent, but perhaps race reports will provide a clue. It is quite possible to spend more time on research than on the painting itself if you are concerned about accuracy.

1962 French Grand Prix – Rouen. American Dan Gurney took Porsche to their first grand prix win on this pretty but challenging circuit. Climbing uphill from Nouveau Monde Hairpin on the backleg of the course, he is followed by Trevor Taylor's Lotus as he sweeps into a left-hand bend under the eyes of the large crowd.

It is always a bonus when it is possible to use a nice setting as the background to a picture of racing cars, and the contrast between such surroundings and the cut and thrust of man and machine make it all the more satisfying. The recession of the converging perspective of the track gives depth to the scene. The front wheel of the Porsche cuts the white line edging the track, and points of contact such as this naturally attract the eye, which in this example is then encouraged to climb up the steps in the bank. Here, the figure of the gendarme leads it along the crowd to the dark tree mass. It is then an easy link to the track, where it follows the line of the cars back to the main subject again, and so on. All of these natural features are points of fact, but with planning it is usually possible to choose a viewpoint which suits the desired purpose, positioning any available incidentals and areas of light and shade to make the best use of them.

1957 Spa 1,000km. Henry Taylor's privately entered D-type Jaguar going through the fast downhill sweep at Burneville ahead of Roy Salvadori's works Aston Martin DBR-1.

Yet another look at the picturesque circuit in the Ardennes, and yet again on a wet day. Quite a rural piece of landscape if we ignore the road and the cars, but we can make use of the position of the buildings to help concentrate our attention on the subject. The link from the light area of sky is made via the white building and the slope of the roof to sweep in the direction of the track to follow the leading car through the bend. When we get to the left-hand edge of the picture, we are led back round by the tree and telegraph pole to the sky where we came in. The point of contact between the trackside white line and the car windscreen establishes the driver as our focal point, which is where our eye will concentrate most of its attention.

1966 French Grand Prix – Reims. Jack Brabham became the first man to win a grand prix in a car of his own construction taking the win after vanquishing the Ferrari challenge. Scarfiotti's car is stopped on the verge at Thillois Hairpin as the driver accepts retirement.

If you can use a well-known feature as a backdrop to the story you want to tell, and if you can fit it all into an acceptable composition, you should end up with a satisfactory picture. Background features can also fulfil the need for some additional point of interest to maintain the viewer's involvement and keep the eye mobile. Be careful, however, to check that the information you have is correct for the period you are depicting, for although a basic circuit layout may remain the same for many years, buildings, bridges, hoardings, grandstands, spectator areas and any number of features can change, robbing your picture of authority if you get it wrong.

1973 German Grand Prix – Nürburgring. The Tyrrell's of Jackie Stewart and Francois Cevert crest the brow of the Flugplatz in the lead on the opening lap, with the rest of the field strung out behind.

The Nürburgring is one of several classic circuits which provide an endless choice of splendid backgrounds, and the distant view across the heavily forested Eifel Mountains from this point is quite spectacular on a clear day. It is usually necessary to show the main subject occupying a major portion of the picture area to satisfy primary interest in the machinery, but it is artistically very rewarding if you can incorporate an attractive landscape as well. It is also very helpful if you can use backgrounds not only to identify the location, but to convey the atmosphere of the surroundings which can vary considerably from place to place and country to country.

Graham Hill, master of Monaco, notches up the first of five wins in the Principality with his BRM in 1963, with John Surtees struggling to maintain contact in the Ferrari as they head down the quayside from the chicane.

Monaco also provides a wonderful variety of attractive settings, and has certainly provided me with more pictorial inspiration than any other circuit. The choice between romantic buildings, exotic gardens or harbourside scenes, with the colourful addition of grandstands full of spectators, is seemingly infinite, but once again be sure to confirm that the details relate to the year you are choosing to portray. This harbourside view gives an opportunity to show the blue Mediterranean waters, and you will probably by now be able to spot the compositional leads such as the iron bollard and the position of the rescue launch blocking the way out on the right.

1972 British Grand Prix – Silverstone. The opening lap at Stowe Corner, with the field streaming down Hangar Straight in the wake of Jackie Stewart's Tyrrell and Clay Reggazoni's Ferrari.

If Monaco is scenically tops as race tracks go, then Silverstone has to be near the bottom, but it is improving now that some artificial bumps and hollows have been constructed. Nevertheless, while making it harder for the artist or photographer to come up with an attractive background, it is possible to make something out of what little there is. Choosing a location where there is a structure such as a grandstand to relieve the flatness of the landscape, plus a marquee to add flavour, is a big help. Even a primitive and rather vulnerable looking marshals' post can be called in to advantage, but it is a much more challenging task. Such period pictures provide an interesting comparison with the same spot today.

1936 Italian Grand Prix – Monza. Tazio Nuvolari defeats the might of the German Auto Union team to win on home ground.

Chicanes were introduced at that time which provided some interesting layouts of straw bales and striped kerbs, and opportunities such as this, although limited to specific periods, do make for unusual and fascinating pictures.

Mexico, and the 1952 Carrera PanAmericana marathon. The winning Mercedes-Benz 300SL of Kling and Klenk hurries along a typical rough road during this mechanically and physically exhausting event.

The cacti and Mexican Caballero add a touch of local colour to establish the nature and typical surroundings encountered during the event, and the dramatic sky helps to glamorize the setting. Incidentally, the background setting and figure references used here both came from a world travel book.

Le Mans 1988 – Jaguar made it back to the winners' circle again, ending the long-time Porsche dominance of the event. Here, the winning car toughs it out with a works Porsche at full chat down the Mulsanne Straight.

Speeds down the Mulsanne are awesome, and the landmark which most people associate with the famous straight is the Restaurant Les Hunaudieres. It provides an interesting background feature in this scene, but is something which can be studied at leisure and recorded at any time of the year if you happen to be passing, for future use. The only addition for the race is the extensive run of Armco barrier. As I have already mentioned, it is often possible to check up on circuit references while travelling, to accumulate useful information and establish the surroundings, both current and historic, particularly where the track utilises public roads as at Le Mans.

Goodwood – the start of the main event at the first race meeting after the war at this delightful Sussex venue. The front row Maserati of Duncan Hamilton and ERA of David Hampshire are joined by winner Reg Parnell in the new 4CLT Maserati and Cuth Harrison's ERA as they get away. Bob Gerard's ERA, which finished a very close second, is behind Harrrison.

A nostalgic reconstruction of the scene, built up from contemporary photographs which show the enthusiastic spectators crowding every available vantage point, haystacks next to the track and refreshingly uninhibited officials and photographers. I was there as a spectating schoolboy, so can recall the excitement and conditions from first hand, although memories from so long ago do need refreshing with reliable confirmation. Available photographs from the period are rather sparse, but it should be possible to glean enough information to piece together an accurate representation.

1979 East African Safari Rally. Shekhar Mehta wins a tough event for Datsun.

As with the picture of the Carrera PanAmericana, long distance events such as this can give some scope for artistic licence in the use of appealing bits of typical landscape, which can be manipulated within reasonable limits without causing a hail of criticism. Colours and skies are of course different in other parts of the world, so be sure to find out as much as you can about countries you have not visited. Travel brochures can be very useful in this respect.

Shelsley Walsh Hill-climb. Bill Ainscough nears the top of the hill in his 'Nurburg' Frazer Nash.

A typical scene in the lovely Worcestershire countryside at a Vintage Sports Car Club meeting. The sight, sound and smell of vintage machinery in a vintage setting is the antithesis of the high-tech clinical atmosphere of modern professional circuit racing. Competence at landscape painting is at a premium here as it is hard to ignore the background. This painting is something of a study in green, but it is interesting how many variations of this colour are present in any such scene. These events, in common with the growing number of historic racing car meetings, provide unmatchable opportunities for close involvement and study of wonderful machines.

Sports cars on the beautiful Montjuich Park circuit outside Barcelona, with Jo Bonnier's 2-litre class-winning Lola leading a Chevron through the winding downhill section of the course.

This track was used for several happy years to host the Spanish Grand Prix in the late 1960s and early 1970s, but failed to keep up to the safety standards required for modern Formula One cars. In its time however, it had an appeal similar to Monaco, and is well worth considering when looking for attractive backgrounds from that period.

1991 Le Mans 24 Hours – Mazda's winning car accelerates away from Tertre Rouge and off down the Mulsanne Straight.

Use of cloud shadow helps to break up the expanse of track behind the leading cars, and emphasizes the sunny weather conditions. The whitewashed tree trunks and road sign on the right add a touch of detail interest to the scene, as do the parked rescue vehicles in the distance, with the elevated local ring-road crossing the bridge beyond. Make use of such incidental detail if you can, but don't allow it to impinge on the more important main theme.

Chapter Eleven

Figures

Like most activities, motorsport involves people, and whether they be in large groups of spectators or small groups working around cars in paddock or pits, they will, like backgrounds, inevitably intrude on your interest in the machinery. Unlike machines, which once defined remain the same until physically altered, most of the principal parts of the human body can move in more than one direction, often at the same time as other parts. The package, in our context at least, is mostly covered with clothing, materials which in themselves are flexible and animated by the movement of the limbs within. There are many books which specifically cover the subject of figure drawing and anatomy which you can study, and if you wish to include people in your pictures it is useful if you have some appreciation of their construction and how the main parts move in relation to each other. However, a few pointers will perhaps be helpful in the short term, and you will find that a basic 'stick-person' is a useful frame on which to build, and not too difficult to construct in an appropriate pose. It then only needs to be 'fleshed-out' to give it a more human appearance, but the most difficult bit is the convincing application of clothing. You may be able to get friends or relatives to pose for you, but moving figures generate movement in clothing, and the best source of good reference is in photographs of people doing things. Draw from such reference, but at the same time try to imagine the position of the body within, and notice the way material folds, flaps and hangs, changing as the point of contact with it alters.

The average adult male figure is eight heads tall, and a quick check on this will tell you whether you have this proportion correct. A standing figure has a centre of gravity which is vertically below the head. As the weight is shifted from one side to another, the head will move correspondingly as the centre of gravity shifts. The centre of gravity of a moving figure is constantly changing, but the head provides the key to the placing of the rest of the body's bulk while this balance is disturbed. In extreme motion, such as running fast, and jumping, the head is not over the centre of gravity, the body relying on momentum and leg and arm motion to maintain balance and avoid falling over. Imagining yourself carrying out the movement you want to portray will help, and if you have a full-length mirror it can be useful to confirm most positions of a less extreme nature by studying your reflection and making a mental note of how things look.

The driver in a modern racing car is hardly visible apart from a rather anonymous helmet and the tops of gloved hands, but remember there really is someone in there. The head inside the helmet is actually supported by a neck on a body, and the gloved hands are on arms which are connected to shoulders.

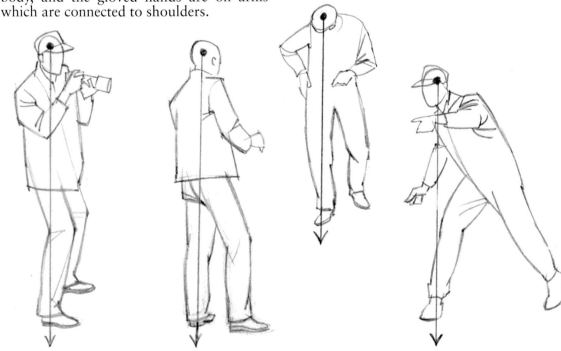

Figures

A montage of female figures from the 1970s.

Cameos of such incidentals make interesting notes which can be incorporated in future pictures, or constitute appealing sketches in their own right.

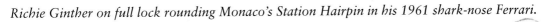

Richie Ginther on full lock rounding Monaco's Station Hairpin in his 1961 shark-nose Ferrari.

A study of a particular racing car can often be expanded to advantage by the addition of a figure or two. In this case, we can identify Fangio and Ascari as suitable companions for the Super Squalo Ferrari of 1955.

Below, the personality takes precedence over the machine at a pre-war Brooklands meeting, with petite and glamorous Kay Petre adjusting her footwear before racing her Austin 750 single-seater.

Figures provide the action in this busy pit-stop scene from the 1962 Six Hours of Brands Hatch for saloon cars. Equipe Endeavour owner Tommy Sopwith controls the stop with the aid of a megaphone, and driver Mike Parkes stands by for a spell at the wheel as mechanics complete the refuelling, brake-pad and wheel change.

Note the wooden box supporting the pneumatic inbuilt jacks. A large charcoal drawing, highlighted with white.

ERAs receive attention in the paddock at a historic race meeting. The clothing of the figures gives away the fact that this is not a pre-war scene.

Grand prix pit stop – a pencil sketch of the Brabham team in action in 1985 depicting the beginnings of the sophisticated high-tech refuelling techniques which are now such an important part of Formula One racing.

'Williams' Bugatti.

1964 Le Mans. A dramatic Sunday afternoon pit stop for the leading Ecurie Belge Ferrari 250LM, temporarily disabled by a thrown tread on the offside rear wheel which has destroyed the adjacent rear bodywork. As the distraught pit crew rush into action, the second-placed Ferrari 250LM goes past into the lead which it held until the end.

The placing of the figures should reflect their importance to the situation or contribute to the action. In some cases the characters have to be recognizable, which can be a problem if they are only small and when a single brush stroke can make a big difference to the appearance of a face.

Louis Chevrolet's Frontenac.

1972 East African Safari Rally – the Porsche 911 of Zasada and Bien passes a group of curious locals.

Used in conjunction with an interesting sky and typical landscape, figures can add to the appeal of an otherwise ordinary portrait of a speeding car, particularly when no other competitors are in sight.

Chapter Twelve

On the spot sketching

While your main source of reference will probably come from photographs, there is no substitute for live, on the spot sketching. This will not only serve as a means for better understanding of the subject, but can also provide information of details and features which are not always clear from shadowy or brightly lit areas in photographs. When setting out to sketch, particularly in relatively crowded situations, it is important to keep your equipment to a minimum. A small sketchpad and two or three pencils, a sharp pocketknife and perhaps a rubber should suffice, together with a large pocket or a shoulder bag to keep them in. If you are able to settle for any length of time by your subject, a small portable stool can be useful, but generally racing cars in paddocks are likely to be moved frequently and are often surrounded by people. This necessitates a flexible approach to sketching which is more conducive to quick thumbnails than detailed studies, so your legs will most probably have to provide support as well as mobility. This also means that you will have to hold your sketchpad in your hand or rest it on your arm, hence the need to restrict the size to something easily manageable.

Try to work quickly, bearing in mind that for one reason or another the time available for any one sketch may be cut short without notice, so use the time to record the important items first, and their position and scale relative to each other, before filling in peripheral details. Establish the position of principle components as lightly as possible and check before committing to more strongly stated tones. Much valuable time can be wasted if you

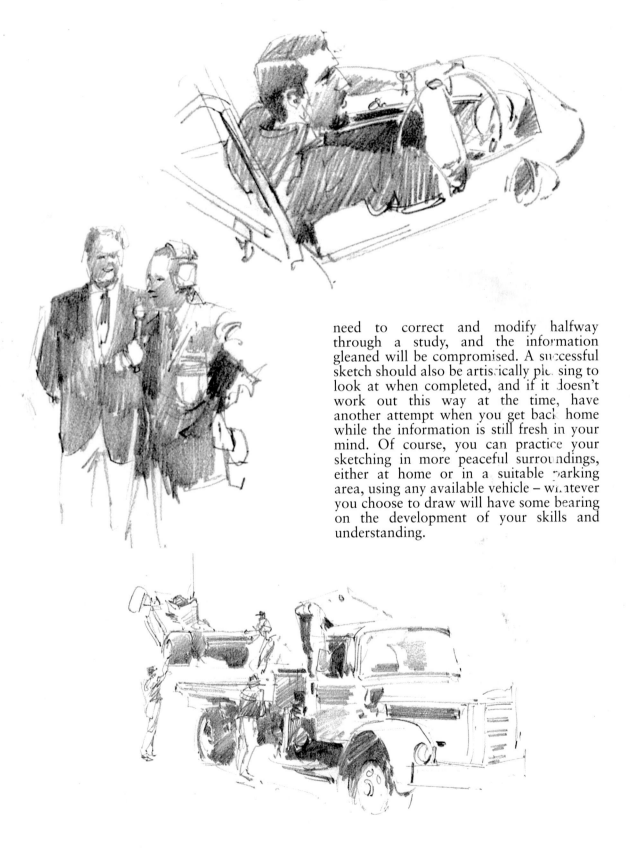

need to correct and modify halfway through a study, and the information gleaned will be compromised. A successful sketch should also be artistically pleasing to look at when completed, and if it doesn't work out this way at the time, have another attempt when you get back home while the information is still fresh in your mind. Of course, you can practice your sketching in more peaceful surroundings, either at home or in a suitable parking area, using any available vehicle – whatever you choose to draw will have some bearing on the development of your skills and understanding.

When confronted by a highly detailed and comprehensive subject, and you have a reasonable amount of time at your disposal without the likelihood of being disturbed, annotate your drawing with notes about colours, and reminders of points of interest, as in the working sketch of the BMC Competitions Department in the 1960s. If, as in this case, photography was not an acceptable option, the information recorded has to be fairly comprehensive if it is to serve as the basis for a painting. However, even when making quick sketches of a fleeting nature, such annotations are worthwhile particularly as reminders of colour details.

Pit stop for a works Alfetta – Silverstone 1950.

Ferrari on a trailer – 1970.
Lotus team mechanics at work – 1965.

If time is really limited, particularly when people are doing things and unable or unwilling to hold a pose for you, a quick outline to establish the basics will have to suffice. You can add tone later if you wish to expand the idea, or use it simply as a reminder for possible incorporation in the future.

If there is plenty of time to sketch something in a quiet corner, you can enjoy the luxury by making a more finished drawing, but always be prepared for the frustration of someone coming along to disturb the scene – their need is usually more pressing than yours.

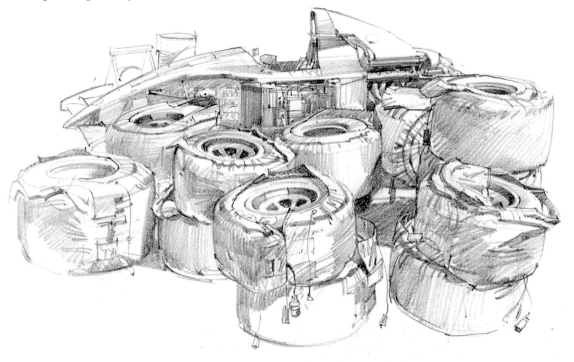

On the spot sketching

Lotus – 1970.
Shadow – 1973.

Chapter Thirteen

Painting materials and equipment

There are a number of different media available to the artist when working in colour. The principle ones which we all know are oils and watercolours, the former generally being associated with canvas, and the latter with paper. Both are usually applied with brushes. Two alternatives which relate roughly to each of these are acrylic and gouache, both are quick drying, and whereas gouache is similar in many ways to watercolour and is used on paper surfaces, acrylic can be used on pretty well anything, and is a useful alternative to oils on canvas.

My own approach to painting an exciting and instant subject such as motorsport dictates that I seek a medium which is flexible but quick drying and suitable for obtaining crisp detail where required. For me, oils are slow to work with, messy and smelly, needing time for cleaning brushes and palette at the end of each session, so the advent of acrylic paint, which I can use on canvas to produce a similar result far more quickly and cleanly, was something of a blessing. There are shortcomings, of course, and the very quick drying nature of the pigment does impose penalties, but to me this is a far lesser problem than that of slow drying oil. I also like to work through a painting as quickly as possible while the excitement is alive, and the drying out periods between sessions of oil painting can induce the risk of waning enthusiasm. This is not to condemn the use of oils, as they might well suit your approach and temperament, but it is worth thinking about before investing in expensive materials.

Watercolour as a medium is clean and relatively inexpensive, but for me too lacking in body to be suitable for the interpretation of such a gutsy subject as motor racing. Gouache, which also uses water as its medium, provides an ideal alternative for me, with opaque pigment which can be washed on thinly or built up into strong passages, and softened or blended as the work progresses. It also allows corrections to be made if handled confidently, and seems to embody the best characteristics of oils and watercolours. On the debit side, as with watercolours, gouache is vulnerable to atmosphere and the attentions of greasy fingers and dust, and when exhibited or hung the finished work needs to be protected behind glass. Acrylics on the other hand are fairly indestructible, and when used on canvas can be framed and displayed to look just like an oil, with no protective glass to reflect surroundings.

Gouache, or Designers Colour as it is commercially known, is supplied in tubes. If you are unfamiliar with it, try first with a limited palette of perhaps seven colours – Permanent White, Prussian Blue, Cobalt Blue, Yellow Ochre, Burnt Umber, Spectrum Yellow and Flame Red. You don't need expensive sable brushes, but good quality man-made bristles as used in Daler 'Dalon' or Pro-arte 'Prolene' will do the job adequately. You will need something to mix your colours on, and an old china meat plate with a flat rim will do nicely, plus a jam jar to put your water in, and some blotting paper to absorb excess water from your brushes.

You can work on watercolour paper, or watercolour board, which is the same stuff pre-mounted on thick card which can be painted on straight away. In either case you will need a drawing board to work on. Some old telephone books make a good prop to position this at a comfortable angle on a table top. If you choose the first option, a medium weight paper with a moderately textured surface is a good starting point, but if you simply use drawing pins to secure it to the board and apply wet colour, the surface will flex and cockle as you work. Not helpful. To avoid this, you must stretch the paper on to the drawing board by first soaking it in a wash basin or, for larger sizes, in the bath. Place in a cold-water dip until both sides are good and wet (about ten minutes), drain off the surplus on removal and lay it flat on the board, taping it down along the edges with gummed brown parcel tape with a good overlap. As the paper dries, it will stretch tight, so if not well secured it will pull away and have to be done again.

Watercolour boards generally come in large sizes, and you will still need a drawing board to work on, but if convenience is a factor these are ideal because, as I have said, they are ready to use with no preparation to do. However, they are more expensive than unmounted paper, so if you are experimenting I recommend you cut the board into smaller pieces, as this will limit the cost if you should end up throwing a few early attempts in the bin.

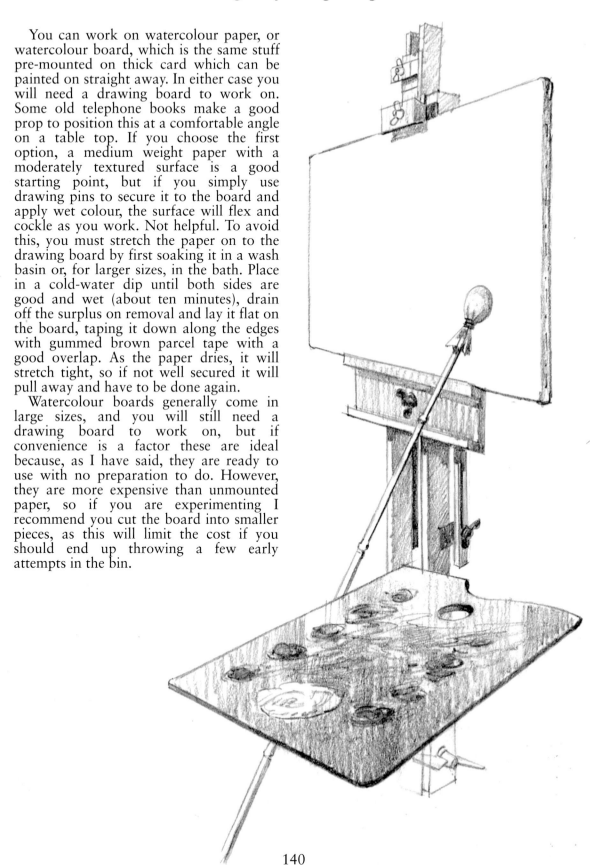

Acrylics are also supplied in tubes, but you will need a flat impervious board to mix your colours on. You can use these colours on most surfaces, including watercolour boards and papers, but if you are going to use them on canvas you will need an easel, a palette, a jar for water, blotting paper or rag, and a mahlstick. These items, apart from the water jar and blotting paper, are applicable to oils too, but with acrylics your palette needs a disposable surface because when dry the paint cannot be successfully cleaned off as with oils, and good wooden palettes are not cheap to replace. You can get tear-off palettes specifically made with acrylics in mind, but I use an oil palette with a sheet of self-adhesive clear plastic, cut from a roll to fit. This can be stripped off and replaced with fresh when necessary.

A mahlstick is a length of (usually) bamboo cane with one end padded. This is held in the same hand as the palette, and the padded end is rested on the canvas to steady your painting hand on. This is necessary because, unlike when working on a sloping board, your hand has nothing to rest upon, and apart from becoming very tiring on the arm, even a steady hand will waver when held in space, making any attempt to put in details pretty unsatisfactory.

The same type of brushes can be used for watercolour, gouache or acrylics, and these can be either pointed or flat ended. Sizes of brushes with conventional pointed shapes are denoted numerically, and as you will only need a small selection to start with I suggest a number 2, 4 and 6, together with some with square-shaped brushes known as 'flats', identified by the measurement across the bristles. Those with 3/8in, 1/2in, 1in and 11/2in flats, or their metric equivalents, will be useful for covering broader areas. If you get on satisfactorily, you will need other sizes and more than one of some, but if cost is a factor, then you will be able at least to test the water, if you will pardon the pun, with the small selection suggested.

If you want to try oils, you will need hogs-hair or equivalent bristles, normally made with longer handles so you can stand back a bit while working, and an oil dipper

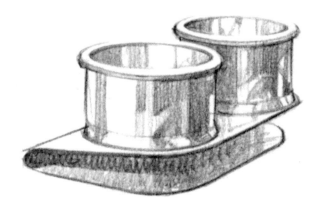

Double dipper

to attach to the palette to hold your medium. There are several media to choose from, but initially you will find distilled turpentine quite adequate. Synthetic bristle brushes can also be used if you are thinning the oil with plenty of medium, but they will tend to clog-up and be too flexible if you try to use oil pigments more generously. You will have to clean the brushes after use with clean turps or soap and water unless you want to throw them away next day. If you value your clothes, wear an overall or something you will not get in a twist over when they inevitably get paint-stained. More generally, you will find a container for brushes handy, and any adequate sized pot will do.

There are, of course, other colour mediums, including pastels, crayons and markers. The first two, while admirable for many subjects, do not easily lend themselves to illustrating complex mechanical subjects. Chalks and pastels can however be usefully employed in conjunction with watercolour or gouache painting, particularly when creating the rough and dusty surfaces associated with rallying and early dirt road racing, so keep an open mind until you have tried them out.

Felt-tipped markers are used extensively in automotive styling, and can be very effective for dramatic and colourful sketching, but there are limitations with the materials most suited to their characteristics, being fairly flimsy in substance, so we will not dwell on them here.

Chapter Fourteen

Applying colour

Watercolour and gouache have several similarities, but for the purposes of this book on painting racing cars, I will confine myself to the use of gouache, the medium I personally favour of these two. We will deal with acrylics and oils later in this section.

Before starting to paint, you will of course have to have some idea as to the content of your painting. If this is your first attempt with colour, I suggest you keep it fairly simple. Before launching into a comprehensive scene, it would be worth spending a little time just playing with colour washes and getting the feel of the paint and the way it flows with varying amounts of water. See how the colours run into each other and how different densities of colour mix affects handling. If you have drawn out a chosen subject, this should ideally have been done on thin layout paper. By rubbing soft pencil on the back of the sheet, you can transfer the outlines by placing it on your paper or board and going over the outlines of the shapes with a pencil (not too soft) or a ball pen. Apply enough pressure to transfer the guidelines, but try not to indent the paper surface below. If you tape the top of the layout paper along the top of the board, you will be able to lift it to check that all you need has been transferred successfully to the paper before removing it. If, as often happens, you see that you have missed a line or two, the layout paper can be flipped down again in the same position to complete the transfer.

Remove the layout paper, and you will have the principal shapes marked lightly on the surface of your board or paper. When you start to apply colour, you will cover up these lines, so if you wish, you can go over

142

the important ones with a fine permanent marker which will show through initially, but make sure it is one which will not bleed under the paint. Try to avoid using markers

Working sketch for 1998 Monaco Grand Prix painting.

where the paint is likely to be thin or lightly coloured, in backgrounds for instance, as it is sometimes difficult to obscure them. More importantly, use them to define suspension arms, air intakes and basic body shapes. Alternatively, you can leave the layout paper taped to the top of the board, and flap it over to reinstate obscured details when necessary.

Having set up your drawing board with a jar of fresh water alongside and a piece of blotting paper handy, you are ready to start painting. Well, almost. You will need to squeeze some paint out of the tubes around the lip of the palette or plate. Put the white out first, at the point nearest to you, and space the other colours out on either side. Until you form your own preferences, and to avoid unnecessary initial expense, limit your palette to the few basic colours mentioned in the previous section. You will have noticed that I didn't include black in the basic colour suggestions. This is because there is no black in the spectrum, and you should be able to achieve a dark enough tone without it by mixing other colours together. However, I have to concede that, to get a good solid dark tone in strong shadows, at the base of tyres and for the insides of air intakes for instance, it can be a useful addition to the palette when mixed sparingly with other colours.

As a general rule, I first wash in the background, starting at the top and working down until all the white paper is covered. Extend your painting a bit beyond the designated border, as it is difficult to be sure you have covered the area you need to end up with as you work. If you prefer, you can put a border of masking tape down to work up to, but you will still need to allow a little extra to be lost behind mount or frame when the picture is finished. You will need to work fairly quickly, and don't worry about painting background washes over the main subject area. Your background will not have continuity if you try to paint round these shapes. If you want the top section to stay wet longer, put a wash of clear water across the paper before putting the colour down, but remember that, with the slope of the board, the colours will tend to run down and collect at the bottom, or run off on to your best

carpet if you use excessive dilutions. While still damp, you can introduce some shape and tone to clouds, trees, etc., using a thicker mix of colour, allowing the shapes to bleed into each other to avoid unwanted hard edges. Adding white will tone down the lighter hues in the sky, and towards the horizon, warm blues will often contain a hint of pink. Avoid using pure white, as even bright clouds have some tone, and remember that gouache tends to dry a little lighter than it appears when wet.

As soon as you can, put in some of the major dark areas, as these will help you establish a tonal balance and assess the light and mid-tones. It is a good idea to finish the sky, if there is any, and distant background tones early, as from here on it is a question of working progressively over the whole picture, defining the shapes and features by applying more paint and blending it into what you already have. Gouache is a fairly forgiving medium, and can be treated quite roughly. If necessary, you can 'blot-off' an area which has gone wrong, or got muddy with too much colour, and go over it with fresh paint. You can also go over with a damp clean brush in parts where the blurring of edges and backgrounds will help to give the impression of movement, or to blend in corrected passages. Build up the foreground car as you go, leaving suspensions, numbers and decals until last. Save your pure white only for the brightest highlights – those pinpoints of reflected sunlight for instance – and never use it in large dollops.

The progress of a painting

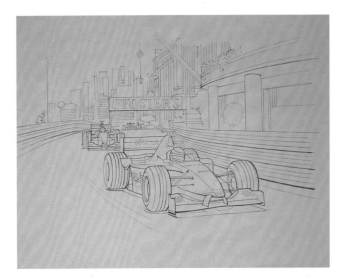

First washes of colour applied in broad areas – try to cover white board with tone as quickly as possible.

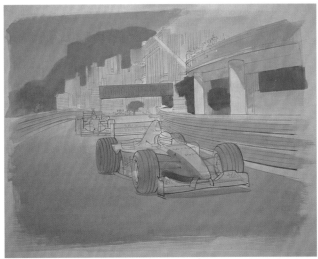

Establish tonal values working on basic washes.

Drawing and painting racing cars

Start adding form and detail progressively.

Develop tone and detail in main subject in line with general progression.

Background and secondary detail such as spectators can be blocked in very simply at this stage.

Applying colour

More detail and refinement – attend to secondary areas and objects.

Picture continuing development overall – details on cars – decals etc now in place.

Background figures also defined in more recognisable form – but don't go too far and get bogged down in too much detail.

Final touches to main subject before you sign off the completed work.

(Painting reproduced by kind permission of The Automobile Club de Monaco.)

1998 Monaco Grand Prix. Mika Hakkinen's winning McLaren-Mercedes leads team-mate David Coulthard as they approach Casino Square.

There is a limit to the practical size you can work to with gouache or watercolour, primarily governed by the largest sizes of paper and board available, but in any case, it is difficult to get the best out of the medium in sizes over 30in x 20in (750mm x 500mm). For larger work, it is therefore necessary to use a different medium, and the natural choices are either oils or acrylics.

Acrylics can be used in much the same way as gouache, but they are not as pliable because once dry, you cannot revive them, soften edges or blend more colour into them. They are also rather thin in their initial coverage of an unpainted surface, but when they reach the stage of adequate covering, they fairly quickly lose their transparency and get progressively darker as more paint is applied. There is a limit to how much white you can add to counteract this tendency, because this creates a pasty or milky dullness to the colour, so you have to be aware of this before it becomes too late. Your Le Mans afternoon scene might have to be amended to a dusk impression if things get out of control!

As with gouache, cover the blank canvas as quickly as possible, start at the top and work down. You will almost certainly need to go over the first application again, so you can correct colours and tones on the second pass. Again, as with gouache, build up colour and definition as you progress from background to main subject, and again save the finer details until last. There are ways of keeping acrylics fluid longer by mixing in a retarding medium, but I personally find this to be an aggravation. A moderate application of clear water

through an atomising spray on the area you want to keep alive for a limited time is perhaps a better alternative, but don't allow water to run down the canvas. This can dry into streaks which leave water marks that have an annoying tendency to show through any number of subsequent applications of colour.

Oils are in this respect easier to work with and blend without becoming progressively darker, but they do get stickier the longer you continue, and they can get quite messy if you don't call it a day soon enough. In contrast with retardants to slow the drying process in acrylics, there are media which you can mix with oil paints to accelerate drying. While I find these equally tiresome, they still leave the colours workable for a reasonable time whilst making it possible to resume work the following day, but you have to adopt a slightly more localised working method to adapt to this facility. If you do try oils, use a 'double dipper' on the palette to carry your medium. Distilled turps is fairly cheap and quite adequate, so use one dipper to clean your brush before mixing more colour using medium from the other dipper, which will otherwise get thick and mucky quite quickly.

The cost of stretched and primed canvas is considerable, so you can if you wish experiment on hardboard primed with emulsion paint for either acrylics or oils. You can use the smooth or the nobbly side, the latter giving a better 'tooth' to work on. Oils can of course be used in thick satisfying chunks if this takes your fancy, and certainly there are times when this approach can be effective, if costly.

Chapter Fifteen

Reference material

The fast-moving environment of the racing car makes it almost impossible to study in detail when in action, but regrettably the opportunity to study Formula One cars at rest is a virtual non-starter for most people these days because of the restrictions imposed on access to all but a very few. The lesser formulae still provide some opportunities for closer study of the machinery, but thankfully, historic events offer the enthusiast ample scope for walking amongst the cars in the paddock and sketching or accumulating useful reference. I have already mentioned the use of reference photographs in relation to figures, and photographs will in the main provide the information you seek when embarking on a painting or drawing. This is equally true where backgrounds and settings are concerned, and the accumulation of pictures which give a good overall representation of a circuit will be well worthwhile. This is particularly necessary when dealing with tracks which are no longer in use for racing, but for the current Formula One scene, television coverage can be another useful source of information. The layout of the venue, colour and location of advertising hoardings, marshals' posts, pit lanes and sometimes even a wider view of the surroundings can at least be analysed to provide some useful ideas. Regrettably, none of these second-hand sources will provide a satisfactory substitute for the experience of being there, but they have to be the best alternative. As with current television coverage, videos and film of historic events can provide inspiration, reviving memories or creating impressions of events past.

Magazines and books will however offer the prime source of car reference, but beware the distortion of the telephoto or wide-angle lens, a necessary tool of the photographer at most current race tracks. It is a common trap when using a photograph as the basis of a picture to place it out of context, where the disparity between the perspective operating in the original setting and distance from viewer makes it incompatible with its new situation. With your ability to construct a drawing to suit your chosen viewpoint, you can interpret and adapt the information contained in photographs, so check that the perspective and viewpoint are in keeping with that of your surrounding scene, and modify as necessary. Whatever you do, don't copy a photograph slavishly, for apart from probably infringing someone's copyright, there is little artistic satisfaction to be gleaned this way. By all means use photographs as a convenient way of practicing the creation of three-dimensional representations of cars, and experimenting and developing techniques with various media. Select details from portions of photos which can be incorporated to the benefit of your composition, but use your skills to combine various sources of information to serve your own creative innovation. Even changing the lighting can transform the impact of an otherwise unexceptional scene, but you should always consider the actual conditions of lighting and weather when recording a specific event.

The camera is a very useful tool for the motorsport artist, and, while sketching on the spot when time and circumstances allow is the best way to hone your skills and improve your powers of observation, there is no shame in taking your own photographs for reference. Certainly you will record far more information this way, and it is also a good idea to back up your sketching with a photograph so that you can complete a drawing later if your subject is moved away before you have finished. I would stress again however that you should use your references in a creative way, and never copy them imitatively without understanding their form.

Drawing and painting racing cars

magazines ...

... books

Chapter Sixteen

Presentation and framing

It is often surprising to note that a good painting is let down by the way it is presented and framed. If you have spent a good deal of time and effort producing what you consider a worthwhile piece of art, it deserves to be shown off to its best advantage. Whether you are intending to exhibit your picture in an exhibition, or just showing it to friends, the reaction will be enhanced by the overall appearance of the package.

Gouache and watercolour paintings will normally require a card mount to set them off properly, and if you are going to use a frame this also serves to keep the picture glass away from the surface of the painting or drawing. Drawings also benefit from the use of a mount in the same way if you want to display them.

It is fairly simple to cut a mount from card to fit around a painting or drawing. Mounting boards can be obtained from your local art supplier, and usually have a white side and a tinted side. Measure the size of the image you want to display, then, using a set square and a robust steel ruler of adequate length, mark up the card to allow a suitable border width. Cut carefully along the lines with a Stanley knife with a sharp blade – but do watch your fingers on the hand holding the ruler – fingertips are very vulnerable and not easy to replace. Place the mount over the piece of work so that the area you want to see is correctly positioned, then stick the back of the piece to the back of the mount with masking tape. It is usually quite effective to use a coloured or tinted card for the border on pencil drawings.

When a painting is framed professionally there will be a choice of frame mouldings and a selection of mount colours available. If it is a gouache or watercolour work requiring a mount. If doing this yourself you can save time by placing pieces of straight white paper or card around the picture first, and deciding the best size and position to suit the content before visiting the framer. Don't be squeamish about masking off a portion of picture just because it has paint on it – anything which detracts from the overall balance must go. There is a choice of clear glass or non-reflective glass, and while it is sometimes tempting to go for the latter in order to avoid reflections, I find it destroys the appeal of an original painting by flattening out the tones and colours to the extent that you could mistake the picture for a print. Surprisingly, those reflections are not usually as much of a problem as they seem, and are more than compensated for by the crisp and satisfying result that only an original can bring.

Canvases present no such problem if you have used the available area properly – there isn't any surplus around the edges, and all you have to do is choose the frame. Make sure it is adequate in size – a large picture shouldn't be spoiled by a skimpy frame. Most framers are happy to give their advice, but don't be persuaded to choose one with which you are not happy.

Chapter Seventeen

Applications and outlets

If you are painting and drawing for your own pleasure, your horizons may not extend beyond the confines of your own satisfaction, and perhaps the possibility of exhibiting your efforts in a local art show at some point. The comments in the previous chapter about presentation will therefore suffice, and you will only have to cast around for an opportunity to submit work when the mood takes you.

However, should you feel the need to demonstrate and share your talents for a wider appreciation, a good starting point to find out how you stand before setting your sights would be an organisation where artists both professional and amateur meet to share their enthusiasm and knowledge, exchange ideas and provide opportunities for comparing and exhibiting work. In the UK there is the Guild of Motoring Artists, and in the USA, the American Society of Automobile Artists, with similar groups to be found in Europe. There are art societies and local art clubs in most towns, and although these do not generally have a particular interest in racing cars, they will give opportunities for more general studies and you will benefit from mixing with people with a common appreciation of art. Evening classes run by local authorities are another way of developing your artistic skills, and you can usually choose the particular speciality you wish to concentrate on, although again you are unlikely to find automotive or motorsport art specified on the curriculum. Membership of an art society or club does of course afford the opportunity of exhibiting your work at whatever shows are organised, and this can provide valuable practical experience. Try not to be too snotty about a muted reaction to your specialist enthusiasm – as I have mentioned earlier, you should try to foster a wide span of competence for the overall benefit of your work.

If your intention is to explore the commercial market, then there are a number of options you might wish to investigate. When I started my professional career, there was an extensive demand for artists able to create competent representations of manufactured goods, including motor vehicles, for use in advertising. Although this market only partly satisfied the need to paint pictures of cars because the products in most cases were passenger cars and commercial vehicles, it did provide a sound financial base on which to build a market for paintings of racing cars. Sadly, for artists, creative photography took over this source of bread and butter completely in a short period of time in the early 1960s, so new avenues needed to be discovered to sustain anything approaching an adequate source of income for the aspiring motorsport artist.

Fortunately, simultaneous with the decline in demand for artwork in advertising, public interest and awareness of art in the area of motoring has blossomed in line with the immense growth of interest in the sport in recent years, and there are opportunities to be tapped now which were not previously available. The most obvious of these is in the demand for art prints from paintings of motorsport events, and the outlets for suitable pictures is through publishers of prints, galleries and mail order specialists. If you are sufficiently confident in the quality of your work, you might consider publishing and marketing your efforts yourself, but this is a very unpredictable business, and requires a considerable financial outlay for not only the production of suitable prints, but their advertising and marketing as well, and is a venture not to be contemplated lightly as a first step or an easy source of even basic life sustaining income.

There are not many publishers who include motorsport in their portfolio, and those who do are probably already fully committed to the relatively few established artists, but if you are considering presenting work to a publisher, make sure your work has neat, clean mounts where appropriate, and put them into a respectable folder or portfolio, not a parcel of taped up brown paper. Good professional looking presentation to a potential client is half the battle, but don't take framed paintings to show, at least initially, unless your approach is to an art gallery. As a back-up to original artwork, publishers would rather see good colour prints contained in a book or album or on sheets of card, or colour transparencies of a decent size, (5in x 4in is usually suitable). These should be displayed in card mounts suitable for viewing on a light box if available, or if you prefer to be forearmed, you could obtain your own portable battery or mains powered light box just in case.

In addition to print publishers, book and magazine publishers are also potential outlets for artwork, but funding is usually a problem for all but the biggest, so make your initial approaches to coffee-table book and part-work houses.

There has always been a market for good original paintings amongst the considerable number of drivers and entrants who compete in the many different categories of motorsport, and for whom a good record of themselves or their cars in action would be an interesting prospect. The pursuit of this type of work by attending events and promoting yourself will require a great deal of application and time, together with an ability to absorb the indignity of rejection, but this is the reality of life whatever the enterprise. You may be able to employ the services of an agent or manager to take on this function on your behalf, but they will of course require a percentage commission on sales. This may be an unattractive proposition, but is perhaps a more acceptable alternative to that of exposing a sensitive nature to the pain and distress of rebuttle.

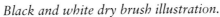

Black and white dry brush illustration.

155

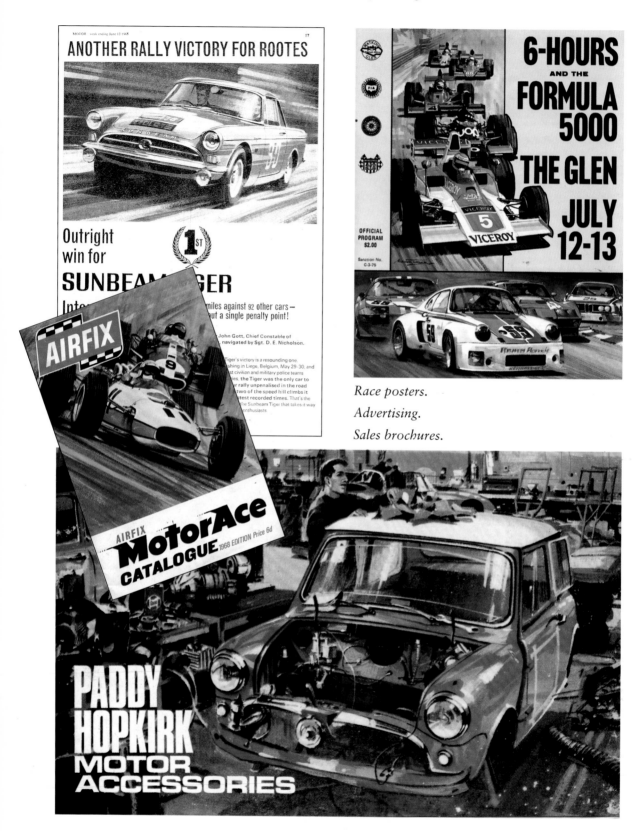

Race posters.

Advertising.

Sales brochures.

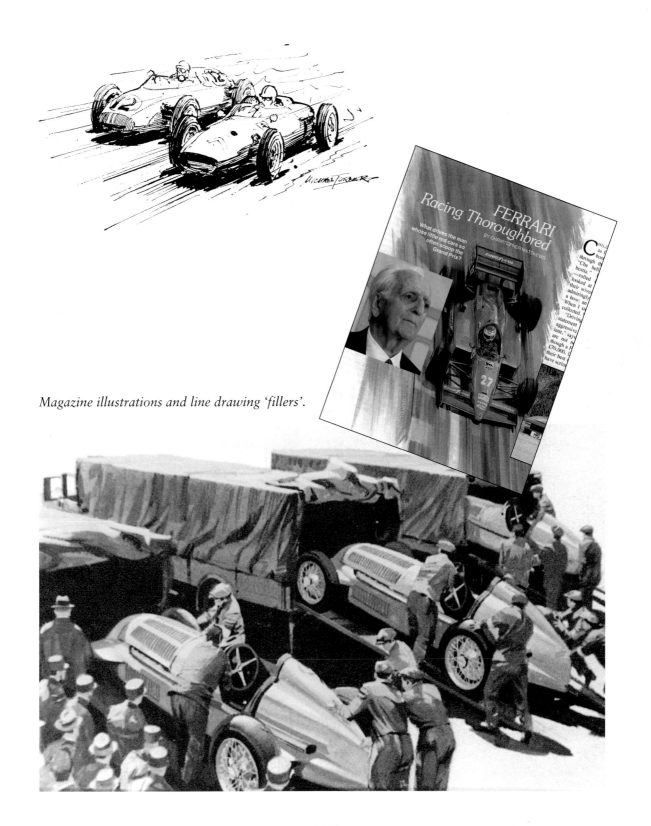

Magazine illustrations and line drawing 'fillers'.

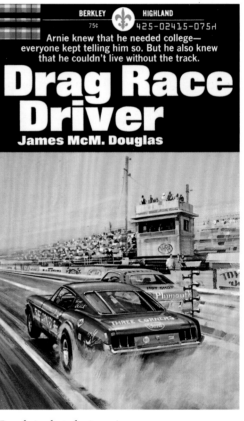

Book jacket design.

Book illustration.

The principle aim should be, when all is considered, to enjoy exploring your talents and the satisfaction of drawing and painting this exciting and stimulating sport at whatever level you choose. There is a lot of pleasure to be enjoyed if you are content to restrict your efforts to those of a hobby, but if this book helps you to achieve pleasure, either in the doing or in a better understanding and enjoyment of other's efforts, then it will have served its purpose.

Index